# PERI PHRASES™
## *for the*
# SALES CALL

## second edition

**Hundreds of Ready-to-Use Phrases for
Persuading Customers to Buy Any Product or Service**

### Jeb Brooks and William T. Brooks

New York  Chicago  San Francisco  Lisbon  London  Madrid  Mexico City
Milan  New Delhi  San Juan  Seoul  Singapore  Sydney  Toronto

The *McGraw·Hill* Companies

7  8  9  0  QFR   21  20  19  18  17

ISBN 978-0-07-174504-8
MHID      0-07-174504-1

**Library of Congress Cataloging-Publication Data**

Brooks, Jeb.
   Perfect phrases for the sales call : hundreds of ready-to-use phrases for persuading customers to buy any product or service / by Jeb Brooks, William Brooks. – 2nd ed.
      p. cm.
   Rev. ed. of: Perfect phrases for the sales call / William T. Brooks. c2006.
   ISBN 978-0-07-174504-8 (alk. paper)
   1. Selling. 2. Sales management. I. Brooks, Williams T., 1945-
   II. Brooks, William T., 1945- Perfect phrases for the sales call. III. Title
      HF5438.25.B7453 2011
      658.85—DC22

                                                                2010026271

This is a *CWL Publishing Enterprises book* created for McGraw-Hill by CWL Publishing Enterprises, Inc., Madison, Wisconsin, www.cwlpub.com

McGraw-Hill books are available at special quantity discounts to use as premiums and sales promotions, or for use in corporate training programs. To contact a representative, please e-mail us at bulksales@mcgraw-hill.com

This book is printed on acid-free paper.

# Contents

# Contents

# Contents

# Contents

# Contents

# Preface to the Second Edition

The world of selling has changed dramatically. And there are lots of reasons for the shift.

- International competition
- Technology
- A shrinking world economy
- Intensified price pressure
- The commoditization of products and services
- Faster communication

These have all combined to make sales an even more demanding career than ever before. However, despite these changes, there will always be a need for salespeople to spend time building relationships with prospects. Let there be little doubt: the world of selling has changed—and changed forever. In all likelihood, it will change even more as the future unfolds. But the real question is: What does that mean for you?

- People have more information than ever before.
- Prospects can get information about you and your offering before you have the chance to present your message.
- You have less time to get your prospects' attention.
- More salespeople are vying for the same prospects' and customers' business.

- Prospects' attention spans are shorter.
- You face more barriers that stand between you and your prospects.
- You need to differentiate yourself from everyone else who sells the same product or service you sell.
- Your margin for error is getting smaller every day.
- You must be willing to change, grow, and study your craft now more than ever before.

If you are to sell well, you can never forget that selling is all about persuasion. However, persuasion is not about your ability to speak for a long time without taking a breath or letting your prospect speak. Instead, it's all about how you can efficiently and succinctly provide solutions that specifically address a prospect's unique set of problems. More importantly, it's how you help your prospects address whatever problems or issues they're facing and the end results you help them achieve.

However, don't for one second believe that it's all about memorizing a set of canned responses. Instead, it's first about understanding the "why" behind every "how." It's gaining a complete understanding of why certain strategies are effective in specific situations. Then, it's all about applying those very same strategies—not word for word, but concept by concept. Don't worry about repeating the phrases exactly. Instead, adapt the concepts—understand and master the subtlety, the nuances, and the key words that are intended in each strategy. As long as you're close, you'll be fine! Just being close is much better than never trying at all. Don't worry about perfection. See what works for you and then move closer and closer to the precise phraseology that's most comfortable and natural for you and most effective with your prospects and customers. You always have to "sound like yourself."

In fact, as you read this book you'll see that we might refer to a strategy (primary bonding statement, statement of intention, etc.) and use different words and phrases for that strategy at different times in the same chapter. That's not a mistake—it's intentional. Except for one phrase (your Direct Value Statement), it's not about memorization—it's about personalization. Personalization means you actually own the words, phrases, and responses that you use. And there's a big difference between memorizing and personalizing!

## Organization

Part One of this book consists of three chapters. The first chapter presents the 12 realities of selling today. It provides you with an overview of exactly why the contents of this book are so critical to your sales success.

Chapter 2 outlines the nine specific sales you'll have to make to yourself before you can ever expect to sell your product or service to any prospect or customer.

The final chapter of Part One demonstrates how you can design and deliver your own Direct Value Statement. We urge you to learn to do this word for word. It will serve you well in lots of situations.

Part Two contains dozens of specific, word-for-word scenarios divided among the six steps of the IMPACT Selling System. These scenarios give you the exact words to use when prospecting, seeking appointments, meeting customers, qualifying and asking questions, making effective presentations, proving your claims, creating value, presenting price, finalizing transactions, seeking referrals, overcoming objectives, and servicing accounts. They can be adapted for telephone, in-person, or e-mail discussions.

Part Two of the book may, at first glance, appear to be the most important to you. And it is important because it reveals the most accurate precise words, approach, strategy, and philosophy for any situation with any prospect. However, don't underestimate the value of Part One, for it's there that you'll find the essential whys behind the hows. In the final analysis, these chapters contain the wisdom that makes all of this work.

Part Three reveals a most powerful, one-of-a-kind set of tools that are being published for the very first time anywhere. Based on years of research, they will reveal the very simple, yet profound reality that prospects rarely buy what they need, that instead they always buy what they want!

In this section of the book you'll find unique research reports that reveal the exact words to use with four types of prospects—the entrepreneur, the corporate executive, the purchasing manager, and the hospital administrator. Those prospects were selected as a representative sample of the prospects to whom salespeople like you must sell. Whether you sell paint to factories, benefit plans to corporations, software to emerging businesses, or medical supplies to doctors, you'll find something relevant here for dealing more effectively with your prospects.

You'll find words to use when describing the relationship that you will forge with each prospect (describing exactly the type of relationship he or she wants to have with a salesperson), the benefits of your product or service (describing them in the exact words he or she wants to hear), the features of your product or service (presented and positioned as he or she wants to buy it), your organization (presented exactly as he or she wants a provider to be), and your price, rate, or fee (described and positioned as he or she wants to perceive it).

## Conclusion

This book has been far more than a presentation of a sales philosophy. Instead, we loaded it with real-world, how-to ideas, phrases, tips, and insider secrets that can propel your sales career instantly.

Again, please take heed of this heartfelt warning. Don't expect the words to jump off the page and work for you. You'll need to read, understand, practice, master, assimilate, and apply them, first in your mind and then with others in safe, nonthreatening environments before you try to use them in the high-risk world of selling. Trust us: They work. However, they certainly won't work if you use them amateurishly, clumsily, casually, or with a false sense of confidence. Also, we will totally guarantee that if you do absolutely nothing they won't work at all. The choice is yours.

You'll need to invest the time required to understand each skill and then use the words and terms as often as possible in risk-free environments. This is one case where practice makes perfect—or at least as perfect as the demanding world of selling can be.

## The Words That Sell Website

Finally, we'd like to leave you with access to a special website (www.thewordsthatsell.com), where many more of the one-of-a-kind tools that are contained in Part Three are available. Access them to transform your sales career. You'll find scores of specialized resources that will empower you to take your knowledge of persuasive communication to levels you never dreamed possible, that will empower you with skills that are far beyond your current level, no matter how experienced you may be. Happy selling!

## Acknowledgments

Obviously, the lion's share of gratitude goes to the book's original author (and my father) Bill Brooks, who passed away in 2007. This is, after all, his book and its revision required only a tweak here and there. He loved everything about sales, and I think his passion for this most noble of professions shines through even today.

I would also like to thank McGraw-Hill and especially John Woods of CWL Publishing Enterprises, who gave me the opportunity to revisit and update this book.

## Preface to the Second Edition

I'm also extraordinarily grateful to Michelle Richardson, Jon Tepper, and Jeff Blackman for taking the time to review the book and provide invaluable feedback.

And finally, I owe a tremendous thank you to everyone at The Brooks Group who provide a marvelous level of service to our clients every day.

# Part One

## The Principles of
## Selling Today

# Chapter 1
# The Realities of Today's Selling Environment

here are 12 realities that form the philosophical under-pinning of why the phrases and terms outlined in this book really work. Why is that? Because sales is a dynamic science that when practiced correctly, becomes an art form. And although its tactics are constantly changing, its foundational principles remain constant.

Let's take a look at a few principles of selling.

## 1. The Secret to Selling Is Never in the Selling

**Reality:** The secret to selling is never in the selling. Instead, it's always in the continuous act of prospecting.

Most salespeople fail because they lack a sufficient supply of qualified prospects. What does that tell you? That you need to consistently, intelligently, and capably prospect for business, no matter how long you've been selling. It never stops. Whether you're vertically integrating an account or attacking an entire market segment, sales is always all about prospecting. And that's true whether you've been selling for two months, two years, or even a lifetime!

## 2. To Sell Successfully, You Must Be in Front of a Qualified Prospect

**Reality:** To sell successfully, you must be in front of a qualified prospect when he or she is ready to buy, not when you need to make a sale.

Because qualified prospects will always choose what they perceive to be the most viable option when making their purchasing decisions, it's essential that you and your company are in front of the people for whom your offering is a viable option. That means qualified prospects! And remember that prospects make buying decisions on their time schedules, not yours. A major part of that secret is to invest your time intelligently and wisely. You must avoid at all costs merely spending, irresponsibly wasting, or just plain abusing your time with unqualified prospects. You need to expediently and efficiently identify the most promising prospects quickly and move beyond those who are not qualified. Your only real asset is time, and your only real advantage is how you invest your time and with whom you invest it.

## 3. You Must Position Yourself Correctly

**Reality:** You must position yourself, your organization, and your product or service correctly in the mind of the buyer.

Due to rapid changes in technology, competitive pressures, a crowded market, and the commoditization of many products or services, you must differentiate what you do and how you do it from the rest of the pack. This is becoming even more critical to long-term sales success. In the final analysis, how you position yourself will far outdistance how your organization, product, or service is positioned. This is true no matter how large or small your organization's advertising and promotion budget may be.

## 4. There Is Less Margin for Error

**Reality:** There is less margin for error than ever before.

This reality mandates that you must always show up on time, fully prepared, equipped with thorough knowledge of your prospects, what they are trying to solve, how they function, how and why they make decisions, and much, much more. Bottom line? Virtually all prospects have a plethora of options from which to choose. Unfortunately for you, you are only one choice among many.

Therefore, you must not only be fast on your feet, but also have the skills to apply your product or service, know exactly how to impart that knowledge to your prospect, and know how you can leverage his or her understanding of it to your best advantage.

## 5. Prospects Must Believe You Have Something Important to Offer

**Reality:** Prospects will only grant appointments to salespeople whom they perceive as having something important to offer that will positively impact them.

Coming across as desperate or ill-prepared will do nothing to help you maximize this principle. On the other hand, knowing what to say and do, when to say and do it, and precisely how to position yourself will allow you to win!

Let there be no doubt. Old-school methods like aimless cold calling, using "tie-down questions," or memorizing scores of worn-out old closes will blow up in your face in this century.

## 6. Being Trusted Is More Important Than Being Liked

**Reality:** Being trusted is far more important than being liked when selling.

Salespeople who master the art of building trust outsell those who are merely glad-handers looking for another target of opportunity. Certainly, in order to have the opportunity to build trust, it's important to be pleasant and friendly. But all in all, a salesperson who is trustworthy and knows how to demonstrate and communicate that trustworthiness at the very first opportunity will outperform one who is just a smooth-talking "flash in the pan." Which do you want to be? Which should you be? Which are you? What type of sales experience are your prospects and customers looking for and expecting? What type of experience do you give them?

## 7. Prospects Are Busy

**Reality:** Prospects are busy.

What does that mean to you? Simply that you need to get to the point of your meeting with the greatest speed and efficiency. Move from small talk to positive, effective sales talk with confidence, trust, and ease. Prospects don't have time to invest in a long, drawn-out journey waiting for you to get to the point.

## 8. Prospects Will Buy to Solve Their Problems, Not Yours

**Reality:** Prospects will buy to solve their problems, not yours.

What might be your problem? To make a sale, earn a commission, win a contest, earn a bonus, keep your job, pay your bills, get a promotion, or look good to other people.

The truth is that none of these have anything to do with their problem! And just what might their problem be? To achieve greater efficiency, make money or a profit, keep their job, fix something that's broken, enhance their organization—or to solve whatever your product or service helps them solve.

## 9. Prospects Will Try to Make Your Product or Service a Commodity

**Reality:** Prospects will try to make your product or service a commodity.

Why will they do that? It's simple. In the world of commoditization, price always rules. Prospects are always trying to get the best price. Therefore, if they can reduce whatever product or service you sell to a commodity, they'll win! Your job is to keep that from happening. However, in order to do that, you must know exactly what, when, and how to deal with it. You need to be prepared to handle "I can get the same thing down the street" and handle it well.

## 10. Prospects Will Want to Know the Price Before You Want to Give It

**Reality:** Prospects will ask the price of your product or service before you're prepared to give it.

Premature price questions are far more the rule than the exception. And, once you offer a price either verbally or in writing, that's likely to be the only thing your prospect will remember about your product or service!

And if you offer it too soon you won't have created value. Why is that? Because you haven't shown how you can satisfy a want, fulfill a need, solve a problem, or resolve an issue.

On the other hand, if you withhold it too long or too clumsily, you'll run the risk of alienating your prospect and creating an adversarial relationship.

Clearly, both of these options are wrong. So, what do you do? Hang on. You'll find out soon.

## 11. Establish Value or It's All About Price

**Reality:** In the absence of value, every transaction revolves around price.

Salespeople (including you) can't presume that prospects perceive, understand, and comprehend the value of any offering without having it first interpreted for them. Price is such a dominant factor in today's crowded marketplace. The value you deliver must be so clear in the mind of the buyer that it supersedes his or her drive to seek a progressively lower and lower price.

## 12. Relationships Have Changed

**Reality:** The nature of relationships has changed forever.

It's true. Customers are not as loyal as they used to be. Couple that with younger and younger buyers coming into the marketplace who have learned to build and manage relationships online, and the impending changes promise to be cataclysmic for the unprepared.

Those factors, the constant pressure to compare prices, and the emergence of new products, suppliers, and services into the marketplace on a wholesale basis all merge to tell us that the terrain that defines relationships has truly been transformed forever.

## Understanding the Realities

All of these harsh realities mean that your fundamental philosophy of sales may need to be modified, as well as the very words, exact phrases, and specific utterances that you've been using. However, there are certain sales truths that have not changed and will likely never change.

For example, the preeminent role customers play in the relationship will never, ever change. In spite of this, there have been thousands of cases where a company or organization had the corner on a market and the employees falsely believed that they didn't need to change, only to discover that once their market changed without them and their customers had other choices, ultimately the customer was still in charge! And those customers decided to change suppliers—fast, furiously, and often.

## Six Truths of Selling

Here are six truths that will never change in the world of selling, no matter how much the landscape of sales may change:

1. Listening is still the best personal skill a salesperson can master.
2. Failing to get in front of the real decision-maker is a fatal error.
3. If you can't close sales, you'll never be successful as a salesperson.
4. Successful selling requires a significant level of skill in time- and self-management.
5. Great salespeople are simultaneously competitive and resilient.
6. Sales is all about presence and persuasion.

This book is really all about number 6. It's about how to create a strong, positive presence and simultaneously be more persuasive. More specifically, it shows you how to be "succinctly persuasive" as well as how to avoid wasting words, time, and your prospect's attention.

Now, let's get to work!

# Chapter 2

# The Nine Sales You Must Make First

Here are the nine specific points you will have to sell to yourself before you can expect to sell your product or service to any prospect.

## 1. If You're Not Sold, No One Else Will Be Either

A lot of work was done during the twentieth century around the concept of "self-talk." That science says that each of us, in the final analysis, is nothing more than a manifestation of everything we have ever heard, read, or believed about ourselves. And that belief is further refined and defined by how we actually utter phrases (usually silently) to ourselves that reflect nothing more than those things we have heard others say, write, or otherwise communicate about us. That is called self-talk. And that self-talk will ultimately define your level of drive, achievement, and motivation. It really is an inside job . . . and anchors your personal level of drive, achievement, and willingness to perform at peak levels.

For example, think about a parent with two children. To one child the parent says, "You'll never be as successful as your sister," and a teacher declares, "You just aren't good in math," while to the other child a parent says, "You'll be great at leading others," and a teacher says, "You have a great deal of potential."

You can guess the result, can't you? The first two create self-doubt, a sense of inadequacy, and a lack of confidence. The latter two do just the opposite. And in both cases, the children start repeating those very same phrases—good or bad—to themselves. And there's a direct relationship to performance.

But what does this have to do specifically with the profession of sales? More specifically, what does it have to do with your view, belief, or the level of confidence you have in your product, service, or organization? In sales as a profession?

Have you ever heard someone say, "All salespeople are crooks," or "Salespeople are people who can't do anything else"? How about this one? "When are you going to get a real job?" Or this gem, "Just promise them anything. Sell it now and we'll worry about fixing it later." Or "I know it's only version 1.0. We can always upgrade or improve it with later versions."

These types of comments plant seeds of doubt in us, forcing each and every one of us to wonder about our profession, our products or services, our abilities, our integrity, and a lot more. And it is essential that salespeople (you!) replace all of this negativity with a more positive bias or point of view.

This can all start with some affirmative, proactive self-talk that enables you to feel more positive, have a clearer and more valuable expectation of yourself and your products or services, and feel better about the organization you represent—to be excited and even grateful—yes, grateful—for what you do, how you do it, and what you have even been placed on this earth to do!

However, it's difficult to use affirmative, proactive self-talk when you are overwhelmed with all types of negativity. What really matters though, is the way you choose to respond to it, how you choose to frame it, and how you choose to define who and what you are. And you do that with positive and productive self-talk, powerful statements or affirmations that you drive into your subconscious. Phrases that deflect, defeat, and reverse the mounds of negativity that come your way about sales, success, your offerings, your self-management skills, and all the negativity that salespeople face day after day.

There's no doubt about it. The first sale that any salesperson must make is to himself or herself. The phrases that you use when talking to yourself are, in fact, the first set of phrases that you will really need to master. We'll deal with that shortly.

You likely opened this book hoping to deal with something else first. Perhaps you wanted to know how to deal with objections, stalls, or put-offs. But if you don't deal with your own sense of direction, self-worth, self-image, and self-belief first, all else will fail. That's precisely why the very first phrases that we dig into are the phrases you need to master in order to sell yourself on yourself and your future, your product or service, and the value that you deliver to your prospects and customers.

It's a basic reality of sales. If you're not sold, no one else will be!

## 2. If You Have No Prospects, You Will Fail

If you have no prospects you'll fail—guaranteed! Prospecting is the key to your sales career.

The single most fundamental reason why most salespeople fail, no matter what they sell, is the lack of a sufficient supply of qualified prospects to whom they can tell their story.

How about you? Have you ever examined your pipeline only to discover that you definitely have too few prospects? Or perhaps you have a lot of prospects—but they really aren't qualified.

Who then, are truly qualified prospects? Truly qualified prospects have five common traits:

- They have a need for your product or service and legitimately want it to solve a problem, fill a gap, give them pleasure, or resolve an issue.
- They have the position, power, and legitimate authority to pay for it.
- They have a legitimate, self-defined sense of urgency to obtain it.
- They have some degree of trust in you, your product or service, and your organization.
- They are eagerly willing to listen to you.

Once you've identified those qualified prospects, you will have to deal with some very specific challenges or unique situations in trying to get face-to-face with them. We'll deal with each of these in detail later. However, now it is essential to stress the importance of the initial interaction that prospects have with you and/or anything about you. That includes your voice, written communication, voice-mail messages, door-opening premium, or anything else that serves as the first interaction between you and a prospect.

Every relationship you'll have with any prospect must start with some interaction. And that first interaction will define the level of receptivity with which that prospect will consider you and whatever you're selling. It will also, in large measure, define the level of trust that will forge your ongoing relationship. Therefore, the first interaction with the right person is essential for you to master. You should define it carefully. It must be accurate. You must think it through thoroughly, and you must execute it flawlessly and with confidence. Anything less is unacceptable and guaranteed to place you in the pile of also-rans who tried their hand at sales and were cast out because they were unable to gain the attention of the right people—the ones who can pay you for your products or services and would, if necessary, move heaven and earth to get what you're selling if you were to present it to them properly.

## 3. Being Trusted Is More Essential Than Being Liked

We talked about this in Chapter 1. Are you fundamentally an approval seeker? Do you say things that you believe allow your prospects to identify with you and you with them? Do you ask them about their collection of antique cars, framed autographs, stuffed fish, or family pictures?

If you do, you'll just be one more face in the crowd. What do you think the last dozen or so salespeople who have entered their office, place of business, or home asked them about? The same things?

How are you different? Asking prospects about the same things makes you the same. For those prospects it makes you a walking, talking stereotype that's the image and style of every salesperson. And that's not good. It makes you nothing more than a "glad-handing approval seeker."

Let me ask you a question. If you had to deal with the same questions about the same things every day, how would you feel? The typical prospect's response to the typical salesperson goes something like this: "They'll start with small talk and then when they think I 'like' them, it's time for them to move to sales talk." Unfortunately for most salespeople, the transition from small talk to sales talk is about as smooth as shifting gears in a car with a defective transmission. On the other hand, the shift from sales talk to small talk is much easier.

Later on we'll deal with the real secrets to avoiding making this first impression. At this point though, it's critical that we discuss the psychology of this whole interaction.

You want to sell. And your prospect wants to avoid being sold—or at least avoid paying your premium price. It's really that simple. And that's what sales is fundamentally all about. However, the prospect may be interested in buying. And that's not double-talk. What I mean is that prospects don't want to be sold. However, they may really want and even need what you're selling. And they want to buy from someone whom they trust, someone who inspires confidence. Quite simply, they merely want to believe that they will receive everything promised to them in exchange for a fair price.

Unfortunately, "glad-handing approval seekers" don't fit that expectation. They may be glib, friendly, and positive, but they don't necessarily come across as being totally trustworthy, 100 percent honorable, or completely professional.

On the other hand, a salesperson who matches the pace and attitude of the prospect, understands what that prospect really wants, allows the prospect to engage in small talk if he or she chooses to do so (but doesn't force it), and allows the process to move at the prospect's pace will generally sell better.

## 4. The Sale Is All in the Questions

A great deal of time is devoted to this topic in this book. The reason? Sales is all about what you ask and hear, not what you say. Unfortunately, most salespeople believe that it's all about the presentation, their ability to be persuasive, the smoothness of their delivery, and the "power of the close." All of this is important. However, what if it's the wrong presentation? What if it's a great presentation to the wrong person? What if it's persuasive, but it persuades someone to make a decision that's not in his or her best interest? What if it's a presentation that falls on deaf ears?

The questions start long before you ever get in front of a prospect. First, you question yourself—and answer the tough questions about the prospect, your presence, and more. Then, you need to ask yourself questions about your product or service. Next, you need to consider the questions your prospect is likely to ask you—and then the questions you'll need to ask your prospect, both before and when you present your product or service. And, ultimately, you'll ask your prospect to buy your product or service.

There are definite questions you must ask yourself as you prepare for your prospect. There are issues on your prospect's mind that you need to be aware of as you first approach him or her. There are questions you need to know to make sure your prospect is ready to hear your presentation. There are questions you'll need to ask to determine what your prospect will buy, when he or she will buy it, and how and under what conditions. There are questions to determine when and how to present your price, justify your case, and ultimately finalize the transaction. Then there are questions you'll need to ask your prospect to secure the purchase.

Yes, sales is all about questions. You know that you really can question your way to the sale, don't you? And it's far easier to do that than to talk your way into it. Another truth? It's not really difficult at all to talk your way out of a sale! Just ask lots of salespeople who do it every day. They sell their product or service . . . and then actually buy it back!

## 5. Selling Is About Providing Solutions

You're not selling products or services. You're offering solutions. Present what you sell so people want to buy.

Let me ask you a critical, foundational question. Do you know the subtle difference between a product-driven presentation and an application-based solution? As obvious as this might sound, lots of salespeople don't really know the difference. And many of those who do, unfortunately, fail to apply that knowledge in the real, rough-and-tumble world of selling.

Oh, they can philosophically discuss "meeting the prospect's needs," "addressing customer concerns," or their "value proposition" with great ease. However, when it's time to make a targeted, prospect-centric presentation, they fall terribly short of the mark.

Earlier I mentioned salespeople who try to sell prospects something rather than allowing them to buy what they legitimately need, want, or would gain the most from acquiring. Have you ever been like that? If so, what drives you and others to do that? A contest? A higher commission? A bonus? Insufficient product knowledge relative to what the prospects really should have purchased? Laziness? Pressure from the boss?

There are lots of reasons to do this wrong—and only one to do it right. And here it is. Your prospects and customers deserve the wisdom of your best, most thoughtful recommendation—a recommendation to help them maximize whatever they're trying to get from your product or service. And for you to fail in that responsibility for whatever personal reasons is simply a failure to understand the essence of professional selling.

And what is that essence? The secret to professional selling is to be in front of a qualified prospect when he or she is ready to buy, and then to present your product or service in such a way that it solves his or her problem, addresses his or her need, or satisfies a want he or she may have. It's that simple.

However, simple isn't always easy, is it? Too many things get in the way. And usually, we're the source or cause of a lot of those things. Here are just a few.

- Ego
- Greed
- A lack of confidence in ourselves or what we're selling
- Failure to actively listen to the prospect

- Believing that we know what's best for the prospect in spite of overwhelming evidence otherwise
- Making false assumptions about the prospect, the conditions, or the circumstances

And there are many more things that get in the way of professional selling.

Selling is really all about presenting your product or service persuasively within the context of how it addresses your prospect's stated, implied, or implicit need, want, or circumstance. Then it is about basing your recommendation on fact and articulating it with persuasion and emotion to create a compelling story that allows your prospect to see, feel, understand, and value your solution. It really is that simple.

## 6. You Can Minimize Stalls, Objections, and Delaying Strategies

"Hey, you've forced me to resist!" Maybe no prospect has ever told you that in just so many words. Yet that feeling is behind stalls, objections, and delaying strategies.

We'll deal with all of these reactions later. Why? Because any book on sales has to have some of that "stuff" in it. However, you want the truth, don't you?

In most cases a prospect will object, stall, or use other delaying strategies only if one or more of these statements are true . . .

- You haven't built sufficient trust.
- You haven't asked the right questions.
- You've asked the right questions but haven't listened to the answers.
- You've presented the wrong solution.
- You've failed to create value that offsets the perception of price.

■ You've moved the prospect through the sales process too fast.

■ Your prospect just doesn't believe the claims you've made.

It's that simple. So, if you want to eliminate such problems, deal with each of the aforementioned issues one at a time as you move through the sale. We show you exactly how to do that shortly.

However, to presume that prospects won't object to things like price, terms, delivery, or conditions would be both irresponsible and naïve. Therefore, you need the tools and skills to contend with the experienced trained buyer who believes that it always boils down to some sort of hand-to-hand (or at least verbal) combat. Yet it's possible to at least minimize the intensity of that combat by applying proper and professional selling strategies before the prospect begins to resist.

Never forget a few critical things in your sales career. Success in sales is all about:

■ Prospecting
■ Pre-call planning
■ Properly positioning yourself and your product or service
■ Building trust
■ Asking the right questions
■ Addressing your prospect's situation with an accurate understanding of what he or she wants to accomplish
■ Creating value
■ Allowing your prospect to feel free to object to anything that causes concern or difficulty

Are objections really a sign of interest? Maybe. At least you haven't been thrown out yet, have you? If your prospect is going to take the time to protest and give you a chance to present your solution again, it would appear that he or she is at least willing to give you another chance. Perhaps the prospect has no other source. Maybe someone told him or her to buy from you, or perhaps he or she feels as if you're the only reliable source. There are lots of reasons to object—and many others to buy. But just remember: at least the prospect hasn't thrown you out—yet.

So, seize the opportunity. Deal with whatever your prospect throws your way. But do it professionally, ethically, and confidently. Learn to manage objections. This book shows you precisely how to do that in a systematic way.

## 7. Closing Is Not Just Using Closes

The key to finalizing transactions is to make prospects happy to buy from you—and then to get them to commit.

Making sales is all about asking people to take advantage of your offer. Remember, if you fail to ask your prospect to buy, you will have accomplished nothing. If you don't make some effort to gain closure, don't expect your prospect to take your product or service of his or her own volition. Closing is essential. No agreement, no sale. No decision to purchase equals a failed effort.

In the grand scheme of things, however, the value of learning scores of closing techniques, memorizing closing phrases, or mastering power closes is far overblown. If you have done everything to this point successfully, finalizing a sale is not, will not, and never should be a major difficulty. So this book contains only one close.

The real secret is to make prospects happy to buy from you. It's an old but proven sales truth that people don't like to be sold. They like to buy. Your job is to make them happy to do that. But never forget: you'll have to ask them to make a decision to do it. And that takes knowledge, skill, tenacity, and frankly, some real old-fashioned courage. And nothing and nobody can give you that courage—not this book or any other, not any motivational speaker, CD, or DVD. You have to get that courage for yourself.

Courage comes from confidence. Confidence comes from preparation. So, it all goes back to preparation and knowledge. And this book can help you in that. Therefore, never forget that because closing sales really is an inside job, you're personally responsible for at least learning how to do it.

## 8. Promise a Lot—and Deliver Even More

Don't, even for one second, believe the old nonsense about "underpromising and overdelivering." To be successful in today's crushingly competitive selling environment you need to give some serious thought to adopting a different philosophy—one that can truly differentiate you from virtually every single competitor.

Here's that philosophy: "Promise a lot but work to deliver even more!"

That means that you actually have to do the things you have committed to doing. It also means that you must have the resources—the delivery, customer service, operational support, etc.—that enable you to do them.

It also means a lot more work on your part: more time, effort, energy, commitment, dedication, and personal follow-through. It means that you can't make a sale and walk away. And that's true no matter what you sell—products, services, processes, or systems. It's incumbent on you, and you alone, to ensure that your customers experience the level of service, confidence, use, and application that you've promised them. You can make the first sale without follow-up strategies. Just don't expect to sell to that prospect again. Make it easier for yourself to keep selling: deliver what you've promised . . . and more!

And never forget one important thing: you're first and foremost your prospects' most critical link to your organization. When things go right, you have a great chance to sell them more.

If things don't go well, you need to bear the brunt of their dismay. The onus is on you to win or lose prospects and to retain or lose customers. And those stakes are too high to risk by being lazy, lethargic, or irresponsible.

## 9. You Must Master Special Situations

There are many unique circumstances that you will have to master if you ever hope to be a super-successful salesperson. And those circumstances center primarily around two specific issues: handling price and dislodging competitors who are already providing products or services to your prospect. Without a doubt, these two issues often prove to be the most difficult for salespeople, no matter their level of experience or expertise.

The first, price, really requires an entire book to explore. In fact, our book *How to Sell at Margins Higher Than Your Competitors*, deals exclusively with this one complex issue. Suffice it to say at this point that your ease in handling the myriad questions and problems that revolve around price will be one of your major challenges. And here's why.

Your continued sales success has a lot to do with margin. Don't believe for one second that you can survive long in the world of sales if you start discounting to meet a competitor's price or in some other way eroding margin. Highly professional salespeople know that the secret to a long-term sales career is how well they deal with price issues and maintain margin despite the efforts of prospects to get them to reduce the price.

The second issue, dislodging a competitor, requires tact, patience, and skill. It involves one of the more subtle and precise skills you will have to master to expand the reach and increase the depth of your sales effort. Ironically, that skill is far more a matter of pre-call planning and intelligent questioning than of persuasion.

One key truth should be both clear and implicit: your best customer is someone else's top prospect! So defend the high ground. And you should simultaneously make someone else's best customer your top prospect, too. That's just the way it is in sales, isn't it?

# Chapter 3
## Your Direct Value Statement

What are the prospecting situations you find yourself in most often? They can likely be broken into the following categories:

- Face-to-face, formally or informally
- By telephone
- At trade shows
- Through referrals from current customers
- Through referrals from people other than customers
- At networking events
- Online

In each of these situations you'll need to know the importance and use of your own, one-of-a kind Direct Value Statement (DVS). Some people call this an "elevator speech." This is a straightforward succinct statement that clearly and declaratively communicates the fundamental reason your organization exists and why you're selling its products or services. And it's likely the most important thing you'll learn in this book. Yet most salespeople never master the concept. In fact, surprisingly, some have never even heard of it.

## Sample Direct Value Statements

■ We assist our clients in the banking industry to improve their profitability. We do this by reducing their costs, improving product performance, and geometrically expanding their markets.

The DVS is such an important concept that we're showing you how to design your own. Why is your DVS so important? Because it succinctly (there's that word again!), clearly, and precisely defines what you do and how you do it. Better yet, it defines clearly "what you do and how you do it" that benefits your customers ... and identifies your core customers. It also plays a central role in virtually every prospecting situation in which you will ever find yourself. In fact, I refer to it in every prospecting scenario explained in this book.

No matter your business, it can always start with the same phrase:

"We assist clients [or customers] in the _____ industry [or business] to _____. We do this by _____."

However, in order to do that, it's important to understand what end-result benefits you actually deliver to your customers. You also need to know what end-result benefits your prospects and customers want to gain, enjoy, achieve, or have.

Here are several examples:

■ We assist our clients [or customers] in the interior design industry provide their clients a wide variety of cost-effective floor coverings. We do this by _____.

■ We assist our clients [or customers] in the real estate industry to pass their state real estate exams easier, faster, and the first time. We do this by _____.

■ We assist our clients [or customers] in the agricultural industry to grow greater yields from their land and enjoy greater profits. We do this by _____.

# Using the Direct Value Statements

Your Direct Value Statement is extremely important. You can use it (as you'll see) for gaining appointments, meeting people, answering the question, "What do you do?" and in lots of other situations.

Again, the structure is always the same:

"We assist our _____ in the _____ industry to _____. We do this by _____."

No matter what your business, venture, service, or industry, this statement will work for you. Therefore, I'd urge you to give some *serious* thought to answering these four questions when developing your own Direct Value Statement.

1. Do you work with individuals, organizations, enterprises, associations, or governments?
2. Do you specialize in an industry? Market? Type of business?
3. What do you help your customers to do? Reduce costs? Improve productivity? Reduce turnover? Maximize returns? Gain market share? Enhance stock value? Improve profits?
4. How do you do that? By improving processes? Improving manufacturing yield? Providing upgraded equipment?

If you cannot communicate the fundamental reason people or organizations choose to do business with you and how you do what you do, you will have a problem prospecting for customers. In fact, if you can't verbalize those things, you'll likely never get your foot in the door.

In the final analysis, people will choose to do business with you to reduce or remove a problem, solve an issue, improve a situation, or enhance their position. They are vitally interested in securing solutions. That's what it is all about.

Some more examples:

- We assist our clients [or customers] in the communication industry to reduce personnel costs. We do this by offering screening and assessment services, hiring systems, and retention programs.
- We assist veterinarians in rural markets. We do this by having the largest research facility in the world with more scientists dedicated solely to large animal care.
- We assist teachers in elementary schools to provide real-time experiences for their students. We do this by having over 300 real-world learning products available at discount prices that we market through home parties for teachers, sponsored by teachers.

Your turn. Fill in the blanks of your value statement.

- We assist _____ [customers] in _____ [industry or occupation] to _____ [how you help]. We do this by _____ [your solution].

Of all the things explained in this book, this one concept could well be the most important to your sales career. Craft your DVS and use it over and over. It will prove to be invaluable to you in gaining appointments with even the most difficult prospects.

More than any other phrase in this book, you must deliver your DVS with ease and confidence. In fact, ideally you should be able to recite it as comfortably as you tell someone your name.

# Part Two

## Scenarios for the Six Steps of the Sale

Part Two presents scenarios that follow the six key steps of the sale, according to the IMPACT Selling System* as outlined below. These scenarios provide the words to use when prospecting, seeking appointments, meeting prospects and customers, qualifying prospects and asking questions, making effective presentations, proving your claims, creating value, presenting price, finalizing transactions, seeking referrals, overcoming objectives, and servicing accounts.

Nobody can provide the exact words for you, of course, because the right words must be appropriate to your products or services and must fit the specific situation with your prospect and his or her words. However, in these scenarios I provide phrases that use effective strategies, and I explain how those strategies work.

There are six steps in the IMPACT Selling System:

**Investigate**—Prospecting, Positioning, Pre-Call Planning
- **Objective:** To pre-call plan, position yourself properly, and gain a face-to-face appointment with a qualified prospect.

---

* The complete IMPACT Selling System is described in detail in *Sales Techniques* by Bill Brooks, McGraw-Hill, 2004.

**Meet**—Building face-to-face trust and rapport
  ■ **Objective:** To set the face-to-face sales process in motion.

**Probe**—Having your prospect identify, verbalize, and discuss his or her needs, wants, and desires
  ■ **Objective:** To determine what, when, how, and why your prospect will buy your product or service.

**Apply**—Showing your prospect how your product or service will solve his or her problem, fill a need, or satisfy a want he or she has verbalized
  ■ **Objective:** To recommend and present your product or service in a way that clearly matches the solution your prospect is trying to achieve.

**Convince**—Corroborating your claims
  ■ **Objective:** To provide powerful social, statistical, or third-party proof of your claims.

**Tie it up**—Finalizing the transaction, cementing, and reinforcing the sale
  ■ **Objective:** To empower your prospect to buy, solidifying the sale, servicing, and vertically integrating the new account.

Clearly, appropriate phrases must fall within the context of each step. I would simply like for you to understand these words, phrases, and series of responses within the larger context of each step in which they are found. That's the foundation of Part Two.

# Chapter 4
# Step 1: Investigate

**B**efore we get into the specifics of the Investigate step, there are some preliminaries to take up that will have relevance for all steps. Let's deal with them now.

## Defeat Negative Self-Talk

We are starting this critical section of this book with phrases related to self-talk for one simple reason. We said earlier that it all starts with you. Remember the reality that we discussed in Chapter 3: If you're not sold, no one else will be, either. Here's how to deal with that essential issue.

Use positive affirmations to convince yourself of your own capabilities, the importance of sales as a profession, and the value of your product, service, or organization. Choose one, two, or three of the phrases from each of the following lists and repeat it or them silently to yourself regularly, up to 30 times each, in the morning and in the evening, over an extended period of time, such as 30 days. Some people find this advice trite or even silly, but it's powerful stuff that works better than you can imagine.

## Defeat Self-Sabotage

This section tells you exactly what to say personally and privately to yourself to defeat self-sabotaging comments you tend to make about yourself, such as "I'll never be wealthy," or "I'll never be successful," or "I'm not worthy of success."

## Positive Affirmations

- I am a capable, confident, professional salesperson.
- I deserve to be successful.
- I achieve my goals and I am fulfilled by what I do.

## Defeat Negative Thoughts About the Sales Profession

The following are statements that you can make to yourself to defeat negative comments relative to your perception of sales as a profession, such as "Sales is not highly regarded as a profession."

## Positive Affirmations

- Sales is an honorable profession worthy of my best efforts.
- Sales is a profession that allows me to create great value for my customers.
- Without me, my customers' most important needs, wants, and desires could never be satisfied.

## Defeat Negative Thoughts About Product/Service

Here are some things you should say to yourself to defeat negative comments relative to your product or service, such as "My product isn't nearly as good as I am asked to represent it as being," or "Our price is way too high for what we offer."

## Positive Affirmations

- My product/service is worth a lot more than I ask my prospects and customers to pay for it.
- My product/service is invaluable to my prospects and customers.
- In the absence of my product/service, my prospects or clients would not be as successful as they need to be.

## Defeat Negative Self-Talk About Your Organization

These are statements that you should make to yourself in order to defeat negative self-talk relative to your organization, such as "My employer doesn't deliver value to our customers."

### Positive Affirmations

- My company and I work hard to ensure we always promise a lot and deliver more.
- My company is well-respected and delivers even more than it promises.
- My employer is the best in our industry.

**Tip:** Select one affirmation from each section (yourself, sales, product/service, and employer/organization), place each on a card that's visible to you at least twice daily, and silently repeat each one up to 30 times a day for 30 days. You'll be surprised at the result, but only if you really believe it will work and you do it daily.

# Prospecting, Positioning, and Pre-Call Planning

In Step 1, gather sufficient information about your market and individual prospects within it to enable you to make the best possible sales presentation

There are four key roles that people can play inside your prospect's organization:

- **Buffer**—the person whose job is to keep you out
- **User**—the person who will use your product or service
- **Check writer**—the person who will approve the purchase
- **Internal advocate**—the person in the organization who can help you

Early in the sales process the internal advocate is the most important person to you. Why is that? That's the person who can guide you through the difficulties you'll inevitably encounter. You'll need to find a way to identify and get in front of this person. And as you'll see, the valuable information you can glean from this person will be critical to you when you get in front of the check writer. The following are questions to which you must uncover the answers early on in the sales process. You need to have the internal advocate provide specific answers to these questions:

- What organization will I be competing against for this business?
- Who is the salesperson I will be competing against?
- How strong a relationship does that person have with the organization?
- How strong a relationship does his/her organization have?
- How long has he/she had those relationships?
- What does the buyer(s) like most about the competition?
- What does the buyer like least?
- What type of time frame is the organization working with to make a decision?
- What type of budget do they have in mind?
- What is their opinion of my company? Our product/service? Me?
- What do they look for in a salesperson?
- What is most important: price, quality, delivery, or service?
- What is the one thing that I could do to lose this sale?
- How is the organization formally structured?
- How does the organization go about making decisions?
- What is the likelihood of change or reorganization within the organization?

- How much depth will I need in the account to ensure that I stay vital?
- What is the single most critical buying motive for the user? For the check writer?

You need to develop such a deep sense of rapport and trust with your internal advocate that he or she will readily, openly, and easily provide you with the answers to these questions.

Just who might this internal advocate be? It might be the buffer, the user, or even the check writer. Bottom line? This is a person inside your targeted organization who sincerely believes that your solution is the best, most ideal alternative for the organization to select.

Equipped with this information, you'll be well-prepared to move forward. Fail to ask these questions and you'll be ill-equipped to know precisely how and exactly when to proceed.

## Appointment-Setting Scenarios

These scenarios are presented in order, from the most effective to the least effective. All are methods for gaining appointments by telephone. There are, of course, other ways (like e-mailing or drop-in cold-calling on an unsuspecting prospect). However, they are far less effective and of significantly less value.

## Your Prospect's Gatekeeper Answers the Phone

**DEALING WITH THE ASSISTANT**

**You hear:** Hello. Bart Decker's office. This is Heidi. How may I help you?

**You say:** Good morning, Heidi. I recently met Bart at [insert event]. He asked me to give him a call, and I promised him I would. I'm wondering if you could connect us?

**You hear:** Certainly.

**You hear:** Hello, this is Bart Decker. May I help you?

**You say:** Hello, Bart. This is _____. We met recently at the _____ where we discussed _____. As you may recall, I indicated that I'd call you and you suggested I do so. Do you have a few minutes right now?

Two possibilities:

**You hear:** No.

**You:** Make an appointment for a call at a more convenient time.

or

**You hear:** Yes.

**You say:** Good. As you recall, I'm with _____. [Insert your Direct Value Statement.] When is a convenient time for us to sit down and discuss how we might help you further?

Three possible answers to this question:

**You hear:** Next week.

**You:** *Schedule an appointment.*

or

**You hear:** I'm not sure.

**You:** *Proceed to ask qualifying questions to have the prospect verbalize a potential problem you can solve.*

or

**You hear:** I'm not interested in this meeting.

**You:** *Proceed to qualify the prospect further to turn the situation around and determine if there is some possible way to meet.*

## You're Calling a Prospect Who's a Direct Referral to You

This usually means someone who knows the prospect has referred you to the prospect. Your prospect's assistant or secretary answers the phone . . .

**You hear:** Good morning. Lester Jamison's office. This is Lori. How may I help you?

**You say:** Good morning, Lori. My name is _____ with _____. Jack Perry, a mutual friend of Lester's and mine, asked me to give him a call and I promised him I would.

There are three possibilities answers:

**You hear:** Mr. Jamison isn't in.

**You say:** I'm sorry that I can't talk with him. However, do you have his schedule so that I can be sure to talk directly with him?

Obtain time frames and set up a firm telephone appointment with gatekeeper. Remember: This is a powerful scenario—you are entering with a referral.

or

**You hear:** Mr. Jamison isn't in. Would you like to leave a message?

**You say:** How would you recommend I do that? Would it be better to leave a message with you or would you suggest that I leave a voice mail?

**Note:** In either case, re-emphasize the asked-promised

phrase when you leave either a message or a voice mail. Remember also that your singular goal is to set up a phone conversation to establish a face-to-face selling situation.

or

**You hear:** Let me check with Mr. Jamison.

Three possibilities can occur:

**You hear:** He doesn't have time to talk with you now.

**You say:** I can understand that. However, do you know if there's a time when he might be available?

or

**You say:** Jack was very eager for me to talk with him. Let me ask you this. Could I send him an e-mail (or drop something in the mail) that he might be able to review? If that's acceptable, I'll call in a week or so to see if he's had a chance to review it. Is that OK?

In this case, it's acceptable to confirm the correct address for sending materials to ensure there's no delay in delivery.

or

**You hear:** He wants to know what this is all about.

**You say:** Please tell him that I have provided some valuable ideas to Mr. Perry, and he felt very strongly that I should talk with Mr. Jamison.

You may be able to get through to your prospect based upon your response to the gatekeeper. If that's the case, be sure to remember that your sole goal is to gain an appointment with your prospect.

If you're asked to send materials, do so. However, try to set a firm time to call again to determine your prospect's response to the materials and to make an appointment.

You get through to the customer . . .

**You hear:** I'll connect you.

**You say:** Thank you very much.

**You hear:** Good morning, this is Lester Jamison.

**You say:** Good morning. As Lori may have told you, my name is _____. Jack Perry asked me to give you a call and I promised him I would.

**You hear:** How is Jack?

**You say:** He's fine  . . . and suggested to me that we have been helpful to him in some ways that may be of interest to you, as well.

**You hear:** What is this all about? or What do you do? or How can I help you?

**You say:** [Insert your Direct Value Statement.]

Again, your sole goal is to secure a face-to-face presentation. You may be able to make an appointment right away based on the power of the referral source. If not, you may want to get permission to forward materials and follow up with another phone call.

# You're Responding to an Inquiry from the Prospect

Such inquiries may come from an e-mail, a request for information on your Web site, a response to a mailing, or even a voice mail message.

Your prospect answers the phone . . .

**You hear:** Hello, this is Doris Maloney.

**You say:** Hello, Ms. Maloney. My name is _____ with _____. I'm calling you in response to your communication with us. As you may recall, you [insert action—called us, left us a message, sent in a response card, etc.] with reference to our [insert your product or service].

**You hear:** Yes, I recall doing that.

**You say:** Good. As you know we [insert your Direct Value Statement]. If you don't mind my asking, is there something in particular that I might be able to help you with?

Your goal here is to get a question that you will answer and then use to lead you to other questions that the prospect wants to have answered.

Then your goal will be one of three: to set a face-to-face appointment, if relevant; to make a phone sales presentation, if appropriate; or to deduce that the prospect is not qualified.

## Follow Up to Set Up an Appointment After You've Sent Materials for Your Prospect to Review

Other than through a prior meeting or a client referral, this is a much more powerful way to approach prospects than through any unsolicited, direct phone, or drop-in attempt.

**SITUATION 1**

You encounter a difficult, resistant gatekeeper.

**You hear:** Good afternoon. Ms. Smithson's office. This is Barbara.

**You say:** Good afternoon, Barbara. My name is _____ with _____. [Insert your Direct Value Statement.] I'm following up on some material I sent last week. I'm wondering if Ms. Smithson is available?

**You hear:** She doesn't take calls from people trying to sell her something.

**You say:** I can understand that. However, I've got a problem and I need your help. Who in your organization handles decisions related to [insert your product or service]?

**You hear:** That would be Ms. Smithson. However, I know she won't take your call. She never does.

**You say:** I do understand. However, maybe you could help me. Do you know if she received the materials I sent?

**You hear either:** (a) Yes, she has; or (b) No, she hasn't; or (c) I don't know.

**You respond by saying either:** (a) Great. If that's the case,

I wonder if I could talk with her about her reaction to what I sent? or (b or c) Let me ask you this. Could I go ahead and forward some new material to her? Perhaps I could follow up next week to see if she has had a chance to review it.

This, unfortunately, is not an unusual or uncommon situation. Many gatekeepers are given the primary duty of keeping you out . . . they are the buffer. Never forget, your goal is simple, straightforward, and clear: to get an appointment with the prospect. Period. Remember, never alienate the gatekeeper. However, if you must, you may need to circumvent that person's role by forwarding material to your prospect and then going directly to a voice mail message, leaving a powerful, benefit-rich statement hoping to either (a) have the prospect eager to expect your next call or (b) have your prospect tell the gatekeeper to anticipate your call.

## SITUATION 2

You have previously forwarded materials for your prospect to review and are now calling to gain an appointment.

**You hear:** Good afternoon. Mr. Price's office. This is Janet speaking. How may I help you?

**You say:** Hello, Janet. My name is _____ with _____. [Insert your Direct Value Statement.] I recently forwarded some materials to Mr. Price about our organization. Do you know if he has received them?

Three possibilities:

**You hear:** I don't know.

**You say:** I sent it last week. I'm wondering if I could talk with Mr. Price to see if he has received it and had a chance to read it. Could you please connect us?

or

**You hear:** Yes, he has.

**You say:** Do you know if he's had a chance to review it? If it's OK with you, I'd like to talk with him to see what he thought of what I sent to him. Could you please connect us?

or

**You hear:** No, he hasn't.

**You say:** I understand. He's extremely busy. I sent it last week. Would you suggest that I resend it? Or do you think that he might have received it without your knowledge? I wonder if you might connect us so that I can track this down?

**Remember:** Your sole goal is to speak directly with your prospect to gain an appointment. The material you sent was to open the door, to provide a reason to have a discussion in order to gain an appointment.

Your secondary goal here, as in all of these scenarios, is to develop an internal advocate as early as possible. Quite often, that person is the gatekeeper. Here's another great phrase:

**You say:** Janet, I'm sure that Mr. Price counts a great deal on you to keep things straight. I'm wondering if you might be able to help me . . . ?

**Never forget:** You need to maximize the opportunity for leverage—to leverage the materials you've sent and your contact with the gatekeeper to determine your prospect's receptivity and to gain access to the prospect in order to establish further dialogue.

## You Haven't Yet Sent Materials to Your Prospect and Are Making a Cold Call

This is, by far, the weakest basis for any contact with any prospect at any time!

**SITUATION 1**

The gatekeeper answers the phone. Her response is positive and receptive. However, when you get to talk with your prospect, he or she shows some resistance and reluctance.

**You hear:** Hello. Margaret Smith's office. This is Barbara. How may I help you?

**You say:** Hello, Barbara. My name is _____ with _____. I'm wondering if Ms. Smith is available?

**You hear:** Yes, she is. May I ask you what this is in reference to?

**You say:** Certainly. As I said, I'm _____. And I'm calling because I'm with _____. [Insert your Direct Value Statement.]

You are connected.

**You hear:** Hello. This is Margaret Smith.

**You say:** Hello, Ms. Smith. As I told Barbara, my name is _____ with _____. [Insert your Direct Value Statement.] I was wondering if it might be possible for us to get together so that I could show you exactly how we could possibly do the same for you.

Pause and wait for a response.

**You hear:** That sounds good. However, I'm not interested

in spending a lot of time looking at what you have to offer right now.

**You say:** I can understand that. My purpose, however, is not to sell you anything—right now, anyway. I'd really like to have a chance to meet you personally, learn something about your situation, and perhaps, give you some idea of what we do so that we might be a viable option for you at a time when you might be interested in moving forward.

**You hear:** I might be willing to listen. However, don't expect me to buy anything.

**You say:** I certainly don't. In fact, I promise that we will only begin a dialogue around taking a look at what we have. I'm wondering—do you have your calendar available? Is there a time next week that's better than any other for us to get together?

**You hear:** How much time will this take?

**You say:** How much time could you spare? I promise I won't take any more time than you can give me.

Establish the time frame and confirm the day, time, and location. Be sure to reinforce that your meeting will take only as long as the prospect can set aside for it. Notice that you respond to a question (How much time will this take?) with a question (How much time can you spare?).

Don't believe that a prospect is or isn't interested in your product or service. Your goal is to deflect his or her belief that you'll expect a purchase decision immediately. Your goal is to emphasize your interest in determining if you can help in any way and to introduce your product or service so he or she will consider it or at least be aware of it. Make sure you never violate that promise. If, however, your prospect becomes interested during your visit, don't hesitate to move ahead as aggressively as necessary.

## SITUATION 2

Your prospect's assistant/secretary answers the phone.

**You hear:** Good morning. Ms. Johnson's office. This is Linda speaking. How may I help you?

**You say:** Hello, Linda. I've got a problem and I need your help. My name is _____, with _____.

**Remember:** Gatekeepers are trained to provide assistance to people who seek it.

**You hear:** How can I help you?

**You say:** As I said, I'm with _____. [Insert your Direct Value Statement.] I would like to talk with Ms. Johnson or send her some information or leave a message with you or leave a voice mail message for her. What would you suggest is the best way to get in touch with her?

Work with the gatekeeper to achieve your one, single objective (an appointment), always soliciting that person's help in suggesting the best way to get your message to the decision-maker.

It's essential that you earn this person's support so that you can broaden your base of internal advocacy within your prospect's organization.

**SITUATION 3**

The gatekeeper answers the phone and the response is positive and receptive.

**You hear:** Margaret Smith's office. This is Barbara. How may I help you?

**You say:** Hello, Barbara. My name is _____ with _____. I'm wondering if Ms. Smith is available?

**You hear:** Yes, she is. May I ask you what this is in reference to?

**You say:** Certainly. As I said, my name is _____. I'm with _____. [Insert your Direct Value Statement.]

You are connected.

**You hear:** Hello. This is Margaret Smith.

**You say:** Hello, Ms. Smith. As I told Barbara, my name is _____ with _____. [Insert your Direct Value Statement.] I was wondering if it might be possible for us to schedule an appointment so that I could show you how we might possibly be able to do the same for you.

Pause and wait for a response.

**You hear:** That sounds interesting.

**You say:** I can promise you this. If it is your opinion that what we have won't work for you, I'll certainly understand and not take too much of your time. Does that make sense?

**You hear:** As long as you do that, I'll be happy to see you.

**You say:** Good. Do you have your calendar handy? If so, let's go ahead and schedule an appointment. Is there a day next week that's particularly good for you?

Agree on a time and date and schedule the appointment.

This situation is not as rare as you may think. There are times when you'll be able to get a good, positive first meeting. It's essential, however, that you remember that your singular goal is always to get an appointment—not to spend a lot of time on the phone and/or make a presentation about your product or service and/or try to make a sale. One more time: your single, primary goal is to gain an appointment.

In many of these situations, you will note the overwhelming importance of your Direct Value Statement. You must prepare it carefully, and it is the only thing in this book that you must learn word for word. Use it at the most appropriate times and it will prove to be invaluable to you.

Should you receive questions with regard to your product or service, always defer them with the statement: I can answer those questions when we get together. However, in order to answer them adequately, I'd like to ask you a few questions to see precisely how our solution can best be positioned to be of greatest value to you when we do get together.

**Never forget:** All phone calls are always about one thing—getting an appointment. You are not making a sales presentation on the phone.

---

**SITUATION 4**

The decision-maker answers the phone.

**You hear:** Good morning, this is Haynes King.

**You say:** Mr. King, how are you today? My name is
_____ with _____. [Insert your Direct Value
Statement.] The purpose of my call is to see if there is
some way that we may be able to get together and
have a discussion about some things that might be of
mutual interest.

**You hear:** I'm not interested in talking to anyone like you.
I don't have the time, the interest, or the inclination.

**You say:** I can understand that. I'm wondering, though, if I
might be able to send you some material that you can
react to and then I'll call, follow up, and see if there's
some way that we might be able to establish a meeting. Does that sound like it might be acceptable to
you?

**You hear:** Yes, that's OK. Just go ahead and send the
material.

Make sure you have the correct address. You can get this
through an online service or additional research. Avoid
having to ask the prospect for the address, especially if he
or she is initially reluctant. The last thing you want to do is
take more time, appear to be disorganized, and come
across as just another cold caller.

**You say:** I'll send you the material today. And if it's OK
with you, I'll give you a call in a few days to make sure
you've received it, and see if you've had a chance to

---

review it. If it looks like it might be of some mutual interest, I'd like to see if you'd be open to setting up a meeting. Will that work for you?

**You hear:** Yes, that's fine.

Your strategy is designed solely to get materials into your prospect's hands because it's clear at this point that trying to talk him or her into a meeting would likely prove to be counterproductive. This process will also give you a reason to make a warm call at a later point as you follow up to ensure the prospect has received the materials and read them, and to ask if he or she has any questions about them.

## SITUATION 5

The decision-maker answers the phone and you receive a positive response.

**You hear:** Good afternoon. Howard Brittain.

**You say:** Mr. Brittain, my name is _____ with _____. [Insert your Direct Value Statement.] The purpose of my call is to discover if you might have an interest in meeting with me to see if there is some way that we could possibly be of service to you.

**You hear:** Well, tell me a little bit more about what it is that you sell.

**You say:** We have worked with lots of organizations such as yours over the years and have found that once we are able to establish a relationship we've been able to assist them in unique and different ways. [Insert your Direct Value Statement.] However, to see if we might be able to be of some service to you, it's important that we have a face-to-face meeting. I'm wondering, is there a time next week that might be best for you?

Your sole strategy here is to gain an appointment, no matter how positive the prospect's response may be. Never place yourself in the position of trying to oversell. You'll note that you never attempt in this conversation to make a sales presentation. You simply talk about the benefits of your particular product or service and establishing an appointment. The biggest mistake you can ever make here is to try to oversell a prospect who seems responsive.

## SITUATION 6

The decision-maker answers the phone and the response is somewhat neutral.

**You hear:** Good afternoon, Jacki Williams.

**You say:** Ms. Williams, my name is _____ with _____. [Insert your Direct Value Statement.] The purpose of my call is to see if we can establish a convenient time to sit down and determine if we might be of some service or value to you and your organization.

**You hear:** Well, I'm not that familiar with your organization and don't know much about it. And, frankly, I'm not sure if we're in a position to make a decision at this point.

**You say:** I can understand that. Very few of our clients are ever in the position to make a decision when we first contact them. However, I would like to send you some material that will give you a better understanding of who we are and what we offer. And then, if possible, I'd like to get back in touch with you in the next couple of days to determine if we might be able to pursue it further if the material looks interesting to you.

**You hear:** Sure, that's OK. Go ahead and send the material.

It's important for you to make sure you have the proper address. Find it online or through some other source. Confirm with the prospect that you'll call in a couple of days to set up an appointment for a meeting.

## Leaving an Effective Voice-Mail Message

This strategy should be used whenever you leave a voice mail message, regardless of how you ended up in voice mail!

You call and are only able to make contact through a voice-mail message.

**You hear:** This is Mary Randolph. I'm sorry that I'm not at my desk right now. Please leave a message and I'll get back with you at my earliest possible convenience.

**You say:** My name is _____ with _____. [Insert your Direct Value Statement.] I'm calling to see whether there is some way that we might be able to be of some service or value to you. I don't expect you to return my call. However, if you'd like to, I'll leave my number. [Leave your number, twice, slowly.] If I don't hear from you in the next couple of days, I trust that you'll be in a position to accept my phone call. So, if I don't hear from you in a day or two, I will certainly give you a call to see if there is some way we might be able to get together.

Never expect your prospect to return a voice message! However, never oversell. Leave a message that is benefit-rich, one that explains in detail the benefits the prospect will receive when doing business with you—your DVS. You'll notice that you give your phone number twice. It's important to do that because the person may not have a pen or pencil handy but can get one by the second time you provide the number. Be sure to give your number very slowly and clearly so that the prospect can understand it. You'll also notice that you're doing your best to establish a situation in which you'll call that person back in a couple of days and he or she will be expecting your call.

You may even want to think about writing your own phone number down as you leave it verbally. Why is that? Because your prospect can't write any faster than you can! Try not to be one of those people who speak at a normal speed until they leave their phone number—and then speed up! Those are the numbers that are easy to delete. Forever.

## Confirming Your Appointment

Never go to any appointment unless you have first called to confirm the time, date, location, and time frame for your meeting. You can do this directly with your prospect or with his or her designated representative.

The reason for this? Why should you waste your valuable time going to an appointment that's not going to happen—that's been postponed or cancelled? Wouldn't you be better off rescheduling that appointment and doing another more valuable activity in that time frame rather than showing up for nothing?

Here's how to do that. First, of course, always do it by telephone. Don't rely on e-mail. Why is that? Prospects, as a rule, won't do anything that requires much extra effort to entertain a sales presentation, no matter how badly they may need or want what you sell. Unfortunately, that's just how it is. Don't expect a return e-mail telling you the meeting needs to be rescheduled. The only exception is the rare proactive prospect who will either call or e-mail to cancel or reschedule. However, don't rely on that. They are few and far between.

**You hear:** Good morning. Ms. Williams's office. This is Corrie. How may I help you?

**You say:** Good morning, Corrie. This is _____ with _____. I'm calling to confirm my appointment with Jacki for tomorrow at 10:00 a.m. I'll be there at 9:45. Our meeting is scheduled for 10:00 a.m. to 11:00 a.m. Is that correct and is everything still on schedule?

Two possibilities:

**You hear:** Yes, it is.

**You say:** Good. I'll see you tomorrow morning at 9:45. Thank you very much.

or

**You hear:** No, there's a problem.

**You say:** I'm sorry to hear that. However, I would like to reschedule, if that's OK. Can you schedule an appointment for me with Jacki or would you recommend that I talk directly to her?

Based on the response, you'll either reschedule the appointment with the assistant or place a follow-up call directly to your prospect to reschedule your meeting.

# Special Situations

At times you may be contacting a person whom you do not believe is a fully qualified prospect.

In the previous prospecting scenarios, you ideally should be calling from a list of qualified prospects or have been referred to a prospect who was somewhat qualified. Unfortunately, however, that's not always the case.

Remember, as described earlier, the ideal prospect for you will have the following characteristics—or at least as many as possible.

1. The prospect has both a need and a want for your product or service—and is aware of that circumstance.
2. The prospect has both the authority and ability to pay for it.
3. The prospect has a sense of urgency about solving a problem or fulfilling a need.
4. The prospect trusts both you and your organization.
5. The prospect is willing to listen to you.

Here's a suggestion. Don't just settle for number 5. How do you do that? You ask the right questions and make the precise, right statements! You can evaluate the prospect on characteristics 1, 2, and 3 by asking specific questions after you tell the prospect who you are and issue your Direct Value Statement. Here's how it works:

**You hear:** Good afternoon. Michelle Richardson's office. This is Robert speaking.

**You say:** Good afternoon, Robert. My name is _____

with _____. We assist our [clients/customers] in the _____ business to _____. We do this by _____. I'm wondering if I might be able to talk with Ms. Richardson about how we might be able to help your organization.

Two possibilities:

**You hear:** I'm sorry she's not available.

**You say:** Would you recommend that I leave a voice-mail message or have you deliver a message to Ms. Richardson?

If the recommendation is to leave a voice-mail message, do it as outlined earlier.

or

**You hear:** Yes, she's available.

**You say:** Good! May I be connected, please?

**You hear:** This is Michelle Richardson.

**You say:** Hello, Ms. Richardson. My name is _____ with _____. How are you?

**You hear:** I'm fine. How are you? How can I help you?

**You say:** I'm fine, too. Thanks. [Insert Value Statement]. I was wondering if we might be able to discuss the possibility of helping you and your organization, as well?

Two possibilities:

**You hear:** Fine.

**You say:** That's good to hear. However, before we go ahead, do you mind if I ask you a few questions so that

I might know exactly how to proceed?

You'll then ask a few of the following questions. Choose the three or four that are most relevant to you and your product or service.

- How familiar are you with our organization?
- How have you been handling any problems relative to [what your product or service solves]?
- How receptive would you be to looking at a possible alternative to your current situation?
- Who normally handles the decisions relative to [your product or service]?
- Who else—other than you, of course—is involved in working with [what your product or service solves]?

The answers to these questions will help you assess how qualified the prospect is at this point. If you determine from the answers to these questions that you should go ahead:

**You say:** It certainly sounds as if we might be able to help you. I'm wondering, could we go ahead and schedule an appointment to pursue this further? Which day this or next week would be best for you?

Schedule an appointment. Call and confirm. Pre-call plan correctly and go to your meeting.

or

**You hear:** I'm not interested.

**You say:** I can understand why you might say that. Lots of our strongest customers haven't been interested initially due to timing, circumstances, or other conditions.

Plus, I'm not trying to sell you anything now. If you don't really need what we have, there's no sense in investing in it, anyway. Isn't that right?

**You hear:** That's right.

**You say:** Do you mind if I ask you just a few questions to see exactly where you stand on a few things? It will only take a few seconds. I promise.

**You hear:** No, I don't mind.

If that's the case, ask a few of the questions outlined in this section to determine whether the prospect has any issues you might be able to help him or her resolve. Then, do your best to schedule an appointment.

If the prospect expresses no interest, do your best to secure permission to contact him or her again at some exact time in the future, put him or her on an e-mail or mailing list, or talk with someone else within his or her organization to gather background information that may help you in case the situation or circumstance changes.

If you determine that the prospect isn't qualified, simply say you appreciate his or her time, but from what you can gather, it wouldn't be to his/her advantage to meet with you and perhaps someone else would be better suited. Thank the prospect for his or her time and move on to the next prospect.

## Dislodging a Competitor

If you're prospecting in an attempt to dislodge a current supplier, the worst thing you can do is to disparage the supplier in any way. There are lots of reasons for that. Among them is that it clearly implies that you believe the prospect has made either a bad decision to hire that competitor or or an equally bad decision in keeping it. In either case, you'll lose!

Therefore, how do you dislodge without destroying your credibility? It starts, of course, in the Investigate step, where you'll need to learn exactly what's going on with the current supplier. The source of information is, of course, your internal advocate.

You'll need to learn from that internal advocate answers to the following questions before you ever get in front of your prospect:

- Who made the original decision to buy from your competitor?
- What were the factors that led to that decision?
- How—if at all—have those factors changed?
- How much loyalty is there to the current supplier?
- Who's the most loyal to them? Why?
- Who's the current salesperson?
- How well is this supplier respected?
- What does this supplier do well?
- What do they do poorly?
- What could be improved, if anything?
- How much interest is there in replacing this supplier?

- What sort of political risks would anyone take in replacing them?
- How receptive is the company to looking at an alternative source?

You'll need to call and schedule an appointment with the right person. You will, of course, need to meet that prospect correctly, as explained in the next step. However, the real secret to this sale is in the Probe step!

You'll need to ask the right questions of the right people within your prospect's organization. Clearly, if there's no problem with the current supplier, if loyalty is strong, and the supplier is providing superior quality or service, you'll be fighting an uphill battle. However, if you've been able to determine that there are some possible chinks in your competitor's armor, you may want to ask the following questions of your prospect in the Probe step:

- If you could change anything about your current supplier what would it be? Why do you say that?
- In looking at your current supplier's performance, how would you rate the following aspects on a scale of 1–10, with 10 being the highest?
  - On-time delivery?
  - Quality?
  - Service?
  - Price?
  - Cost?
  - Support?
  - Responsiveness?
  - Customer service?

- Ease of use?
- Etc.

■ How receptive would you be to having us try a test or trial to see how well we could do?

■ What would determine, from that test, our level of success?

Clearly, the answers to these questions will tell you how qualified this prospect is! There's no sense in trying to dislodge something that can't be dislodged. However, if your pre-call planning research indicates that there is some degree of receptivity toward at least looking at another option, that's a good start.

You need to get in front of the right person and have him or her verbalize some degree of receptivity to change, an openness to pursue other options, or to try some sort of trial or test.

You can then proceed to dislodge! However, proceed with caution. Expect your established competitor to respond. Prepare for the fight of your life. If there's not a fight, perhaps you should wonder why. Maybe they don't care about losing the account. What does that tell you?

# Chapter 5
# Step 2: Meet Your Prospect

**Objective:** To set the face-to-face sales process in motion.

This is the interaction that launches the sales process. It's critical to the sale.

Why is that? Because it establishes the primary perception . . . and you have merely 19–39 seconds to establish that perception as being either positive or negative. Here's how it works:

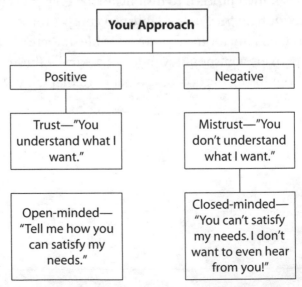

Let's look at the most common ways salespeople tradition-ally open the sale so we can see how the process we're going to explain is so different.

1. Small talk (That's a great pen. Do you collect pens?)
2. Product or service reference (Our product has been fea-tured on TV!)
3. Benefit claim (We can reduce expenses by 30 percent.)
4. Tie-down or provocative question (If I could show you how to double your productivity, you'd be interested, wouldn't you?)
5. Company reference (We're the oldest.)
6. Quality claim (We've been rated #1 in the industry.)

Here's some shocking news. Every one of these traditional ways to open the sale elicits either a negative or a neutral response on the part of prospects. Here's how they rank and the percentage of prospects who feel negative or neutral toward each approach based on our proprietary research with 6,852 decision-makers, which is found in our book *You're Working Too Hard to Make the Sale.*[*]

- Unsolicited small talk (95 percent)
- Benefit claim (89 percent)
- Product or service reference (85 percent)
- Tie-down or provocative question (84 percent)
- Company reference (74 percent)
- Quality claim (71 percent)

So, what is the best way to open the sale?

---

[*] *You're Working Too Hard to Make the Sale* by William T. Brooks and Tom Travisano, Greensboro, NC: GamePlan Press, 2005.

## Statement of Intention and Primary Bonding Statement

We're going to suggest a statement of intention (even though 78 percent of prospects feel either negative or neutral about statements of intention!). However, this strategy, when immediately followed with a primary bonding statement (a statement that offsets any negativity or neutrality), is, in all likelihood, the least risky and the most easily articulated. The bottom line is that you must say something!

However, remember that the exact phrasing of the statement of intention can reduce even further any potentially negative effect. So, here's how you open the meeting with your prospect:

**You say:** Good morning, Bill. I'm _____. It's certainly good to meet you. Thank you for this opportunity.

Then you insert a statement of intention:

**You say:** If it's all right with you, I'd like to use this opportunity to meet you, and for us together to determine whether there's some way that my company and I might be able to be of service to you and your organization. Is that OK with you?

**You hear:** That's fine with me.

**You say:** Good.

Then you insert a generic primary bonding statement:

**You say:** Our real goal here is to help you get what you want. To help us do that, do you mind if I ask you a few questions?

Part Three of this book provides you with the exact primary bonding statement to use with five specific prospect types. However, this generic bonding statement will work with all prospects. Use it!

**You hear:** Fine.

**You say:** I'd like to take a few notes to be sure that I have a record to refer back to. Is that OK with you?

**You hear:** That's OK with me.

That's it! That's all you have to say to initiate the sales process on a positive, productive note. Don't worry about looking for something in the prospect's home or office to discuss (such as mounted fish, paintings, or pictures). Don't be concerned with small talk unless it's initiated by the prospect. Then respond appropriately.

There's an important point to be made here.

**Remember:** I said prospects are bothered by unsolicited small talk. That means small talk you initiate, not small talk they initiate.

Your prospect might ask, for example, How was your drive? or Did you have any trouble finding our place? or How long did it take you to get here?

These comments are clearly attempts by the prospect to engage in small talk. You will, of course, respond and engage in conversation. For example:

**You hear:** How was the drive?

**You say:** It was fine. However, the traffic was a little heavy on Route 45. Is that pretty common?

In this scenario you will, of course, continue to discuss the traffic and whatever other topic comes up. However, your constant goal will be to steer the discussion (at the appropriate time, of course) back to the sequence of statement of intention, primary bonding statement, and permission to ask questions and record answers. And you must stay alert to any opportunity that will allow you to do that.

Remember, your sole goal in the Meet step is to set the face-to-face sales presentation in motion while ensuring that you create a positive primary perception. This is your agenda:

1. Tell your prospect why you're there.
2. Let your prospect know that you want to help him or her get what he or she wants (not what he or she needs).
3. Ensure that your prospect understands you'll need to ask some questions and record the answers. Even with permission to proceed, your success in asking the right questions will hinge totally on your ability to ask even the most difficult questions in an empathetic and caring way, with the right words and tone.
4. Have the prospect acknowledge he or she agrees with this agenda and wants to accomplish the same things.

To achieve this fourth objective, there's an excellent verbal strategy that virtually guarantees your prospect will be comfortable and totally at ease and will answer your probing questions candidly and openly. Here it is:

**You say:** If in the course of our discussion, we mutually discover that I don't have anything that I can help you with, I can certainly recommend someone else who might be able to help you. Does that sound fair?

**You hear:** It certainly does.

**You say:** Good! Then let's get started.

The secret here is for you to be totally committed to referring your prospect to someone else if you discover that your product or service doesn't address the specific issue that your prospect is trying to resolve.

Again, Part Three offers examples of precise, exact primary bonding statements to be used with five types of customers. The next best thing to using those carefully researched phrases is for you to use this generic bonding statement: Our ultimate goal here is to help you get exactly what you want.

The key here is to understand this one simple truth:

**Prospects eagerly buy what they need from salespeople who understand what they want.**

That means that you must assure prospects that you'll help them get what they legitimately want.

Here are some examples of what prospects specifically want, based on their roles:

- Entrepreneurs want independence and freedom.
- Primary care physicians want to practice medicine without outside interference.
- CFOs want no disruptions of their day-to-day work flow.

It's critical for you to understand that saying to a prospect, "I'm here to meet your needs" falls on deaf ears, while, for example, "I'm here to help you achieve your goals" while working behind the scenes (the primary bonding statement for an HR director) elicits a fantastic positive response. And you must accomplish this early in the face-to-face interaction—again, within 19–39 seconds.

Rest assured, however, incorporating the simple phrase "help you get what you want" will usually be more than enough to gain the favor of lots of prospects who are tired of salespeople who dominate the conversation, overstay their welcome, or never get to the point.

Believe it or not, that's all there is to it. Don't make the Meet step more than it needs to be. It should be enough to launch you on what we call "The 90 percent path."

Here's what that means. A negative primary perception gives you perhaps a 10 percent chance of success, while a positive primary perception gives you a greater than 90 percent chance of success. Again, those statistics are from research we conducted for our book, *You're Working Too Hard to Make the Sale.* Which would you choose: 90 percent or 10 percent?

Now, let's go over the sequence one more time:

**You say:** Good morning, Ms. _____. I'm
_____. It's certainly good to meet you. Thanks
for the opportunity.

If it's acceptable to your prospect . . .

**You say:** I'd like to use this opportunity today to meet you, and for us together to determine if there's some way that we may be of service to you and your organization. Is that OK with you [statement of intention]?

**You say:** Our real goal here is to help you get what you

want [generic primary bonding statement]. To do that, do you mind if I ask you a few questions? Is it OK if I take a few notes so that I have a record to refer to?

**You say:** If in the course of our discussion, we mutually discover that I don't have anything I can help you with, I can certainly recommend someone else who might be able to help you. Does that sound fair?

Now, you're in the Probe step.

# Chapter 6
# Step 3: Probe for Success

**Objective:** To have your prospect identify, verbalize, and discuss his or her needs, wants, and desires.

Note the wording: This is the phase of the sale in which the prospect expresses his or her needs, desires, and wishes. Then you determine what he or she will buy, how he or she will buy it, why he or she will buy it, and under what conditions he or she will buy it. Never forget: Different people buy the same things for different reasons—theirs and theirs alone. Not yours. Your goal is to uncover those very personal buying motives.

It's really no big secret that people buy for their reasons and not for yours. This is the fundamental truth behind the Probe. However, the real winning secret behind the Probe is the questions you ask to learn why they really would choose to buy your product or service.

This section provides you with some of those questions. However, the level of success that your sales career will reach ultimately will be determined by your success in learning how to develop your own questions. So, you'll now have that opportunity across a broad array of questions. We'll then take a look at a series of silver bullet questions that will help you sell better, no matter what you sell or to whom you sell it.

# Problem–Resolution Questions

In the final analysis, your prospects will buy your product or service to solve a problem, relieve a situation, or resolve an issue that they have. Period. For example:

- To improve cash flow
- To reduce overhead
- To increase sluggish sales
- To break out of a rut
- To stop being embarrassed by a situation

To understand how to use problem–resolution questions, you'll need to know exactly what problems, situations, difficulties, issues, or circumstances your prospect is likely to want to resolve, eliminate, reduce, or replace. You also need to know what issues your product or service helps them resolve.

So, here's what you do. Ask yourself this question: What problems or issues could this prospect possibly have that your product or service could help remove, relieve, or improve? List those problems on a piece of paper, numbering them from 1–10. Determine what questions you need to ask your prospect to determine if your prospect really does have the problem you've listed.

If you've done proper pre-call planning and research and you've learned from your internal advocate(s), you should ideally already know those problems. Even so, you still must pursue these questions. Why is that? Because it's all about getting the prospect to verbalize the problems, agree that he or she wants to solve them, and commit to a solution.

So, now you have a list of problems and questions. For example:

| Potential Problem | Question |
| --- | --- |
| Reduce manufacturing waste | "How much, if any, manufacturing waste do you currently experience?" |
| Cost overruns | "How often, if ever, do you experience cost overruns?" |
| Poor physical conditioning | "How frequently, if ever, do you feel tired, run down, or have an overall sense of physical weakness?" |
| Inefficiency in kitchen | "How would you rate your ability to get things done quickly and efficiently in your kitchen?" |

## Agitation Questions

Just because someone has a problem, there's no proof that he or she is prepared to take action on it. Therefore, you need to determine exactly how much of a problem your prospect has and how strongly he or she feels about taking action on it.

To determine this, simply ask agitation questions to follow up each problem–resolution question. For example:

**You say:** How much manufacturing waste, if any, do you currently experience?

**You hear:** Quite a bit.

**You say:** If you don't mind my asking, what's quite a bit [agitation question]?

**You hear:** Enough to make a significant difference in our gross profit.

**You say:** How big a problem is that to your profit picture? What will happen if it continues [agitation question]?

As you can imagine, by asking these types of questions you'll learn lots of powerful things you'll be able to use later. Let's take a look at another example:

**You say:** How would you rate your ability to get things done quickly and efficiently in your kitchen?

**You hear:** Well, we're certainly not as productive as we need to be.

**You say:** What sort of problems does this create for your wait staff? Customers? How does it affect the number of tables you can turn each night? What does this mean to your bottom line? Turnover of wait staff? Training time, money, and energy [agitation questions]?

This scenario can be played out with any product, service, or offering. Why? Most people are far more interested in alleviating problems than anything else. However, we're not done yet. There's a third leg to this stool: solution- and feeling-based questions.

## Solution- and Feeling-Based Questions

These questions allow your prospects to tell you exactly how they feel about the current problem(s) and how prepared they are to solve the problem(s). The examples:

**You say:** How do you feel about that?

**You hear:** Not good.

**You say:** What steps, then, if any, have you taken to alleviate the problem?

Customer explains some steps taken.

**You say:** How do you feel about those things? How severely have they affected you so far? What happens if this continues?

**You hear:** I think it could be a problem. I've noticed some morale problems and some customer grumbling. Maybe I ought to start looking into it.

**You say:** What steps, then, have you taken to alleviate the problem?

You'll notice that we've taken the questions to three levels:

1. Problem-resolution questions
2. Agitation questions
3. Solution- and feeling-based questions

This is a process you can use to determine the level of pain from any problem for any prospect, with any product or service, and in any business-to-business or business-to-consumer situation.

Again, here's the formula:

- What problems/pains do you have?
- To what extent is it causing you discomfort?
- How do you feel about it?
- What have you done thus far to solve it?

It's really that simple!

## Needs-Based Questions

If you haven't been able to uncover enough information about the specific problems your prospect is trying to solve through pre-call planning or an initial phone interview, you may want to start the Probe step with needs-based questions.

The reason for this is that needs-based questions are not as potentially intrusive or penetrating as problem-resolution questions. Therefore, they're not nearly as dangerous or potentially volatile. On the other hand, they're not nearly as powerful or revealing. Let's take a look at how to develop needs-based questions.

First, write the name of your product or service on a piece of paper. Then, next to it list those needs that a prospect would likely have for your unique product or service. Some examples are listed below, product by product or service by service:

| Product or Service | Potential Need Product or Service Fills |
|---|---|
| A mortgage | To afford a home |
| An automobile | Transportation |
| Accounting services | Accurate tax information |
| Furniture | To decorate a home |

To do this successfully, you'll need to list at least five to eight specific needs that your product or service can fulfill. Here's an example:

| Product or Service | Potential Need Product or Service Fills |
|---|---|
| Heating and air conditioning repair and check-up service | ▪ To keep equipment running efficiently<br>▪ To ensure that equipment retains value<br>▪ To keep property properly cooled<br>▪ To keep certain objects in home properly cooled<br>▪ To ensure that guests are comfortable |

The next step is very simple. Convert those needs into questions. Using the previous service (air conditioning repair) as an example, here's how that would work.

To determine if the prospect has a need for keeping his or her equipment running efficiently, you might ask . . .

- How long do you usually keep your original heating and air conditioning equipment?
- What experience have you had with equipment that's not maintained properly?

To determine if the prospect has a need for the equipment to keep its value, you might ask . . .

- How familiar are you with the costs of a complete system overhaul? Replacement costs? How long do you plan to live in your home?

To determine if the prospect has a need to keep his or her property properly cooled, you might ask . . .

- How often do you find your [home/office] to be uncomfortable?

To determine if the prospect has a need to keep certain objects properly cooled, you might ask . . .

- What objects, if any, do you have in your home/office that must be kept at 68° or cooler?

To determine if the prospect has a need to be sure guests are comfortable, you might ask . . .

- How often do you entertain out-of-town guests? Have dinner parties?

- If so, where do you do so? Inside or outside?

These are, of course, merely examples for reference. However, they should help you a great deal if you follow the suggested format.

## Feature-Benefit Questions

Would you agree that if a benefit your product or service provides is of no value to your prospect, the feature that drives that benefit is totally worthless to them—no matter what you think of the feature?

If you don't agree, you probably should! The secret, therefore, is to ask questions to determine if your prospect needs a specific benefit that your product or service provides and then present your product or service within those defined parameters.

Let's look at how this works.

| Product or Service | Feature | Benefit |
|---|---|---|
| Flat-screen TV | 2" thick | Takes up less floor space |
| **Question:** "How important is it for you to maximize your available floor space?" | | |
| Floral delivery service | Same-day service | Flowers when and where you need them |
| **Question:** "How often do you need flowers delivered on short notice?" | | |
| Gas generator | Automatic starting | Gives you peace of mind when power is lost |
| **Question:** "How many times a year do you lose power in your home and need immediate electricity?" | | |

To master this questioning skill, you will simply need to

list your products or services, determine the unique set of benefits that each provides, and then prepare questions that answer this one, single question:

**What do I need to ask my prospect to determine if he or she needs each benefit?**

## Objection-Testing Questions

In old-school selling, salespeople were taught to learn canned responses to the most common objections that they'd hear. And because it's so old-school, none of them are included in this book! Over the years lots of books have been written on exactly what words to use when certain objections are heard. If you believe that approach still works, you may want to find some of those old books—they're still around. And most are in mint condition because they haven't been read or used!

It's like the old joke about the prisoners who weren't allowed to speak to one another. However, they would occasionally yell out numbers. Apparently, each number was a joke. One prisoner would yell out "36!" and another would laugh. Then another would yell out "42!" and laughter would ring out again. Apparently, it was a special code—not unlike a sales code for overcoming objections or closing a sale. The "think it over" response or the "Ben Franklin response," for example, were two such memorized strategies. The promise? Just call up the right one and you'll be successful! However, that is not going to work in today's competitive market. I guarantee that. Today's buyers are far too sophisticated for that.

Let's take a different approach. We'll take a look at common objections, and develop a method for managing those and all others through a series of objection-testing questions you can ask in the Probe. The purpose of these questions is to determine two things:

## Step 3: Probe for Success

> 1. Whether an objection will ever come up
> 2. Precisely how to craft your presentation to deal with that objection when you apply your solution

Let's start with this sequence:

**You hear:** I want to think about it [objection].

**You say:** What process do you use when making decisions like this [objection-testing question]?

or

**You say:** What kind of a time frame are you working with to make this decision [objection-testing question]?

Think about this for a moment. If you ask either or both of those questions, won't you have a better, clearer idea of whether or not your prospect will tell you, later on, that he or she wants to think about it? Better yet, if you know that your prospect likes to give extensive thought to decisions, doesn't that tell you exactly how to proceed? Faster or slower, decisively or deliberately, with a simple presentation or multiple presentations? How your prospects answer those two simple questions ensures you'll never hear "I want to think about it" ever again!

Now, let's look at other common objections and some questions you can ask to either avoid them completely or at least be able to anticipate them.

**You hear:** I want to talk this over with _____ [objection].

**You say:** Who else, other than you, of course, is involved in this decision [objection-testing question]?

**You hear:** Your price is too high [objection].

**You say:** What kind of a budget range are you working with?

or

**You say:** What role does price play in your decision [objection-testing question]?

or

**You say:** Which is more essential in your decision—price, quality, or delivery [objection-testing question]?

**You hear:** I'm happy with my current supplier [objection].

**You say:** If you could change anything about your current supplier, what would it be [objection-testing question]?

**You hear:** I'm not ready to make any type of decision [objection].

**You say:** What type of time frame do you have in mind for making this decision [objection-testing question]?

**You hear:** I need to talk with some other suppliers [objection].

**You say:** How broad a search are you conducting for this purchase [objection-testing question]?

or

**You say:** How far along are you? How many potential suppliers, if any, are you planning to talk with [objection-testing question]?

These testing questions allow you to anticipate potential objections, prepare your presentation to deal with them, or position yourself to feel confident they may never come up with this prospect.

## Yes/No Questions

There is a role for yes/no questions. It's to seek clarification of your understanding of a particular position, circumstance, situation, condition, decision, or point of view. However, to be truly valuable, it should ideally be followed immediately by open-ended questions. Here are some examples:

**You say:** Are you pleased with your current level of productivity?

**You hear:** No.

**You say:** That's interesting. If you don't mind my asking, why do you feel that way?

You'll notice that the follow-up or clarification question starts with a statement, such as "That's interesting." The purpose of that type of statement is to demonstrate understanding and empathy or to neutralize the response. Some more examples?

**You say:** Is your current situation going to continue?

**You hear:** Yes.

**You say:** If you don't mind my asking, what impact will that have on your ongoing plan? Are you planning to continue manufacturing that product?

**You hear:** No.

**You say:** Alright. But let me ask you this, if you do discontinue it, what plans do you have for a replacement?

The statement can be a complete sentence or the preface to

a clarification question. Either way will work. The ideal format, however, is to use the yes/no question as a springboard to further clarification. This example shows how to take the questioning down several layers—three layers in this case.

**You say:** Are you planning to expand your fleet?

**You hear:** No, I'm not.

**You say:** Okay. What's driving that decision [level 1]?

**You hear:** We're concerned that the economy is going to weaken.

**You say:** I can understand that. What impact, if any, do you think that will have on the rest of your business [level 2]?

**You hear:** I believe that it will ultimately affect our subsidiaries as well.

**You say:** If that's the case, what impact do you believe that will have with reference to expanding your outsourcing needs [level 3]?

Here's the formula:

- Yes/No question
- Statement or phrase
- Clarification question—level 1
- Clarification question—level 2
- Clarification question—level 3

# Level 1, Level 2, and Level 3 Questions

These types of questions can be used to gain depth in any type of question, not only yes/no questions. After all, it's essential for you to have as much understanding of problems, situations, issues, and circumstances as humanly possible before you present your solution, isn't it?

To use level 1, level 2, and level 3 questions, you simply follow up any question with questions like these:

- That's interesting. Tell me more.
- Why do you say that?
- Could you expand on that a little?
- What are the ramifications of that?
- How would that work for you?
- What further steps would you take?

An example:

**You say:** What is your biggest single challenge right now?

**You hear:** Staying competitive in the market.

**You say:** If you don't mind my asking, what is really driving that competition [level 1]?

**You hear:** Lower-priced competitors. Frankly, they're just driving us to our knees.

**You say:** I understand. Who is your toughest competitor [level 2]?

**You hear:** It's not really one competitor. It's everybody.

**You say:** If you don't mind my asking, what do you mean by "everybody" [level 3]?

Hopefully, you can see that you could go to levels 4, 5, 6, 7, or higher! The secret? It's really nothing more than a conversation. Remember: It's not a monologue! How about another example?

**You say:** What is the single most important issue you face when it comes to a purchase like this?

**You hear:** That's easy. It's the down payment.

**You say:** I see. Let me ask you this. What role does the down payment play in your decision [level 1]?

**You hear:** Well, what do you require?

**You say:** That depends on a number of factors. But I'd like to ask you this, if I might. How important is the length of the loan to you [level 2]?

**You hear:** I haven't really thought about that.

**You say:** That's OK, and not unusual. Most people haven't really thought about it. However, maybe this question would help. What do you plan to do with the property in 8 to 10 years [level 3]?

**You hear:** Why is that important?

**You say:** That will play a big role in the decisions you'll be making relative to building equity. However, if you're not sure about that, I'd like to ask you this . . . [level 4]

This example should show you exactly how to respond to whatever you hear, transition it to another question, and continually get more information relative to developing a solution for your prospect.

## Silver Bullet Questions

Silver bullet questions are ones you can ask almost any prospect, no matter the product or service you sell. I urge you to take them and use them. Mix them with the other eight types of questions we've discussed, and you'll be well on your way!

- What are some of the major challenges/changes in your company/department/industry in the past 6/12/18 months?
- What impact have these had on your profits/morale/market share, etc.?
- What, if anything, are you looking for from an organization like ours that you haven't found?
- What do you like most about your current supplier?
- What, if anything, would you like to see them improve or change?
- What kind of budget range, if any, are you working within?
- What kind of time frame, if any, do you have in mind?
- What have you seen that's particularly appealed to you?
- What process do you use to make this type of decision?
- Who else, other than you, of course, is involved in this decision?
- What is it in your current situation that you don't want to see change?
- If you could change anything about your current situation, what would it be?

- What is the single thing that's most important to you about this type of decision?
- If we were able to solve your problem, what would this mean to your organization?
- What would it mean to you personally?

# Chapter 7
# Step 4: Apply Your Solution

**Objective:** To recommend and present your product or service in a way that clearly matches the solution your prospect is trying to achieve.

The purpose of this step of the sale is to show the prospect precisely how your recommended product or service meets his or her specific needs, solves a problem, or delivers a specific benefit. This is far more than demonstrating your product or service. Instead, it's applying your recommendation as a solution. There's a big difference between the two.

Here's how to transition from Probing to Applying:

**You say:** I understand you're looking for improved efficiency, reduced costs, and maximizing your technology. Is that correct?

You'll have listened carefully to what your prospect has told you he or she is trying to accomplish, solve, eliminate, seek, or resolve. However, you'll have gotten to this point only if you've been able to identify at least three specific solutions you can provide to your prospect. Five would be even stronger. It's critical that you do not move to this point unless you've uncovered especially strong solutions to recommend to your prospect.

Three possibilities:

**You hear:** Yes, that's correct.

**You say:** Based on that, I'd like to recommend . . .

or

**You hear:** No, that's not accurate.

**You say:** I'm sorry. What is it that I missed [or misunderstood]?

or

**You hear:** Yes, but I'd also like to _____.

**You say:** I understand. Is there anything else that you'd like to pursue before we proceed?

If you've consumed a significant amount of time in the Probe, you may want to suggest that you establish a specific time at a later date to return and make your presentation. If so, you must establish a mutually acceptable time, date, and location for that next meeting.

However, if the opportunity is right and time is available to do so, you may want to go ahead and begin your presentation.

## Make Your Recommendation

When you're prepared to recommend a solution to your prospect, be absolutely sure to present it only within the scope of the specific parameters that your prospect has verbalized for the problem that he or she is trying to resolve. This is true whether you're presenting a tangible product, a professional service, or a software solution. Remember: You've previously described your understanding of what your prospect is attempting to accomplish. Now, however, you'll prioritize those things as follows.

**You say:** I understand you're looking to solve _____. Is that correct?

Two possibilities:

**You hear:** No, that's not correct.

**You say:** I'm sorry that I missed that. So, please help me. Could you confirm for me what's the most Important thing you're looking for?

You then reprioritize your presentation, dealing with the number one priority first and then ask your prospect to reconfirm number two, number three, number four, etc.

or

**You hear:** Yes, that's right.

**You say:** Based on what you're trying to accomplish first, let me tell you what I'm going to recommend to address that issue.

Now, present your product or service in such a way that it

specifically addresses your prospect's number one, most pressing issue. For example: "As you can see, the speed of this machine will reduce your downtime by 25 percent. Let me show you how it works . . . . " You then confirm the prospect's second, third, and fourth priorities and work your way through each benefit or feature in their order of importance to your prospect.

# Handle Premature Price Questions

Of all the issues you'll ever face in the sales process, the premature price question is not only the most problematic, but also the most common. I've placed it here in the Apply step because it has to go somewhere. However, don't be shocked if it comes much earlier.

This question can arise in several places. It could come while you're prospecting and seeking an appointment, when you're meeting with the prospect, or here in the Apply step before you've been able to create sufficient value for your product or service. That's because, like you, your prospect doesn't want to invest too much time in something that won't go anywhere. This could involve price, order levels required, delivery dates, etc.

No matter when this question arises or why, if it's asked prematurely, don't answer it! You must always deal with it as outlined in this section.

The problem? If you appear elusive or evasive or if you handle this whole thing clumsily, you're guaranteed to lose the sale. Therefore, you need to know how to handle the inevitable with accuracy.

First, what are the most likely questions you'll hear? They all deal with price, but come in the following formats:

- How much does it cost?
- What's your best price?
- Give me a ballpark price.
- How much is that one over there?
- What's the minimum order required?

- Do you have any up charges?

No matter what the specific question, you need to be able to handle the issue. There are two basic strategies:

- The delay
- The range

### The Delay Strategy

**You hear:** How much is it?

**You say:** We have a full range of prices. However, before we deal with that, let's make sure that it's exactly the right thing for you. Does that make sense?

Two possibilities:

**You hear:** Fine.

Proceed to ask sufficient probing questions to enable you to identify the three to five specific needs or issues you can help your prospect resolve.

or

**You hear:** No, I want to know the price.

Go to the range strategy.

### The Range Strategy

**You hear:** How much is it?

**You say:** We have a full range of prices. However, before we can even deal with that, let's make sure that it's exactly the right thing for you. Does that make sense?

**You hear:** No, I want to know the price.

**You say:** We have a range, anywhere from _____

to _____. No doubt you'll be somewhere in between. However, before we can be more specific I'll need to know more about what you're trying to accomplish. Once I know that, I'll give you the exact price. Does that sound fair?

When you present your range, it's critical to present a bottom price that is, realistically, the lowest possible price you can accept. That's because the low price is likely the only thing your prospect will ever remember about your presentation! Therefore, fail to use this strategy at your own peril!

In most cases, you'll then proceed to say, "To determine that exact price, do you mind if I ask you a few questions?"

In almost all cases, this will satisfy your prospect. However, you'll need to provide your prospect the range of prices you promised and not be afraid to do so.

## Present Your Price

Make no doubt about it: Knowing when and precisely how to present your price is essential to your success in sales. Present your price only after you've created sufficient value to offset the perception of cost and emotional turmoil. Let's deal with that issue now.

### The Stacking Strategy

The best way to do this is by applying the stacking strategy.

**You say:** Before I give you our price, I'd like to make sure that you understand everything that it includes. Is that OK with you?

**You hear:** That's fine with me.

**You say:** Good. Then let's get started.

Everything that will be presented here is for illustrative purposes only. You will, of course, need to substitute your specific information where appropriate.

**You say:** You indicated that you wanted a supplier that could deliver on time, guaranteed. Our price includes that guaranteed on-time delivery and if we don't do that, you'll receive a 10 percent discount. You also wanted the full warranty, dedicated technicians, 24-hour service, and the latest software. Our price does, of course, include all of that. Your major concern was color consistency. Our price also includes our upgraded color-matching system. Our price includes all of this for $5.00 per unit in lots of up to 1,000 per order. But that's not all. We also provide full data backup, easy-to-read billing, and a dedicated account representative to handle any issues that may arise. How does that sound?

Let's take a graphic look at how we just worked the stacking strategy.

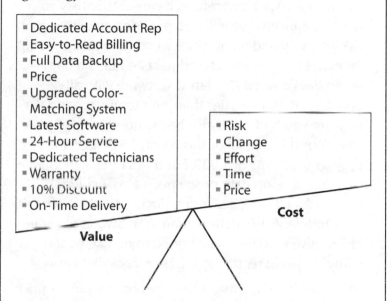

Clearly, the features to be gained outweigh the cost, don't they? However, you can achieve this only by stacking the features—those attributes that clearly outweigh the cost, effort, time, risk, and other issues—that together constitute the cost of your offering in the mind of your prospect. Now, let's make it even better!

**You say:** Before I give you our price, I'd like to make sure that you understand everything that it includes. Is that OK with you?

**You hear:** That's fine with me.

> **You say:** Good, let's get started. You indicated that you
> wanted a supplier that could give you peace of mind
> relative to on-time delivery. We can do that on a guar-
> anteed basis. We will, in fact, even make it more attrac-
> tive with a 10 percent refund if we fail to satisfy your
> delivery concern. We will also provide you with our no-
> risk warranty and technicians who know your account
> intimately whom you can contact 24 hours a day,
> seven days a week. Our latest software with all
> upgrades that are easier than ever to understand—a
> concern you had—will also be included at no extra
> cost. Your price for all of this is only $5.00 per unit, in
> easy-to-order lots of 1,000. But that's not all. To ensure
> that you have no data problems, it also includes
> backup for all data, delivering documents that contain
> easy-to-follow instructions, and your own account rep-
> resentative who will be assigned to handle your most
> complex, yet essential issues. How does that sound?

You'll notice how we "upgraded" the presentation of price
by listing benefits instead of features. Now, our formula
looks like the figure on the next page.

Clearly, we have outweighed any perception of cost by
listing the benefits and "burying" the price between those
benefits. Compare that with the following:

> **You hear:** What's your best price?

> **You say:** Five dollars per unit in lots of 1,000.

What do you think you'll hear? How about this?

> **You hear:** $5? And I have to order 1,000 at a time? Are
> you crazy?

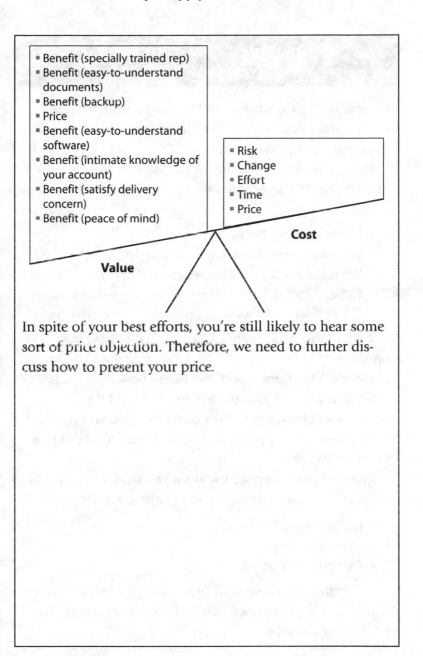

- Benefit (specially trained rep)
- Benefit (easy-to-understand documents)
- Benefit (backup)
- Price
- Benefit (easy-to-understand software)
- Benefit (intimate knowledge of your account)
- Benefit (satisfy delivery concern)
- Benefit (peace of mind)

- Risk
- Change
- Effort
- Time
- Price

**Cost**

**Value**

In spite of your best efforts, you're still likely to hear some sort of price objection. Therefore, we need to further discuss how to present your price.

## Guarantee That Your Price Will Never Be Accepted

There's often great wisdom in knowing exactly what not to do in certain situations. One of those is knowing how *not* to present your price.

First, avoid at all costs any of the self-defeating, even stupid statements salespeople make when presenting price, such as:

- I'll give you my best price.
- I'll really sharpen my pencil on this one for you.
- We really want your business, so tell me where I need to be.
- Do you have your seatbelt on?

Each of these statements is guaranteed to have your prospect drive you to your knees. What do they all communicate? One thing—you don't even believe in your price; that you feel your price is too high and if your prospect will balk, hesitate, or complain, you will panic, retreat, seek a lower price, and do whatever you need to do to secure an order.

The other surefire giveaway is for you to place some sort of modifier on your price as you present it. Some examples?

- Our regular price is . . .
- Our standard price is . . .
- Our quoted price is . . .

What do you believe your prospect will deduce from that? That his or her price will be lower, that's what! That you're negotiable on your price.

The best way to present your price is to say, "Our price is . . . " However, when that price is stacked between benefits, you have clearly created a situation where you have maximized the value that's represented in your price.

Few factors in the sale are more important to your ultimate success than when and how you present your price, so learn how to do it with confidence and power.

## Make the Feature-Benefit Conversion

Remember that in the Probe step I suggested that you ask feature–benefit questions to determine which of the features of your product or service would fit seamlessly into your product or service recommendation and presentation. Here's how to present your solution to your prospect based on those findings.

**You say:** You've indicated that long-lasting wear was important to you, isn't that right?

**You hear:** Yes, I did.

**You say:** Let me explain the construction of our X-19 model, the one I've recommended to you. As you can see it's triple coated and is made of heavy gauge steel. The triple coating means that it'll last longer than any competitor's model. The heavy gauge shell means that it'll withstand more intense pressure than any product on the market. Does that sound like the kind of thing you're looking for?

**You hear:** Yes, it does.

Here's another example:

**You say:** You indicated that the assignment of a senior copywriter is important to you. You also want to run a test of the copy before the full-blown mailing goes out. Isn't that right? Our senior copywriters each have at least 10 years of experience. That means that each and every one has done at least 500 projects like yours. And in our case, if they don't have a 95 percent success rate, they don't stay here! By the same token, each of them has done at least 1,000 split-copy tests during their careers. That means lots of tested, proven experience will be on your team. Does that sound like the kind of experience you're looking for?

**You hear:** It sure does.

## The Power of Course-Correction Questions

When you're presenting your solution, it's essential that you are confident that it's 100 percent, totally on target relative to solving your prospect's most pressing problems, addressing an issue, or resolving a dilemma. To do that, you need to know just exactly where you stand throughout your presentation.

Here's how to do that. As you present your solution, stop and ask your prospect exactly how on or off target your solution is. You do that by asking course-correction questions. Examples?

- How does this look?
- Are we on target?
- Does this look like something you can use?
- Does this make sense?
- How are we doing?
- What do you think?
- Can you see yourself using this?

You'll hear one of three answers when you ask these questions.

Three possibilities:

**You hear:** Yes, I like it.

If your prospect's response is positive, that means that your presentation is on target. Keep going!

or

**You hear:** No, I don't.

**You say:** Why do you say that? How did I miss the target?

**You hear:** I don't like the color.

**You say:** What color would work better for you?

**You hear:** Do you have it in red?

**You say:** Of course we do. Let me show you the same thing in red. How does this look?

**You hear:** That's much better.

Here's another example:

**You say:** How does this look?

**You hear:** I think it's too complicated for our application.

**You say:** What part is too complicated?

**You hear:** We don't need all of the upgrade options.

**You say:** Which specific options, if any, do you feel would be most helpful to you?

**You hear:** Maybe just the Phase I and Phase II options.

**You say:** That's fine. Let me show you how it works with just those options. How does it look now?

**You hear:** That's much better.

The strategy in this scenario consists of doing four things:

1. You ask a course-correction question.
2. You respond to your prospect's answer.
3. You present an alternative solution.
4. You ask another course-correction question to determine if you've correctly realigned your solution.

It's essential to remember to stop frequently during your presentation to make totally sure that you are 100 percent on target. The only way to do that is to ask course-correction questions, and then act according to the response.

or

**You hear:** I'm not sure.

**You say:** What is it that you're not sure about?

**You hear:** I'm not sure about the upgrade option.

**You say:** I can understand that. But if you don't mind my asking, what is it about it that makes you unsure?

**You hear:** It's the cost of the upgrade. I don't think it's worth it.

**You say:** I understand. However, let me tell you what makes it such a great opportunity at the price we're offering . . . .

This is the formula:

1. Ask what the prospect is concerned or unsure about.
2. Listen to his or her answer.
3. Display empathy and then ask a question that allows the prospect to tell you exactly why he or she is concerned or unsure.
4. Listen to his or her answer.
5. Deal with the issue or concern.
6. End your response with a course-correction question, such as "Does this clarify your issue?" or "Does this resolve your concern?"

These questions are essential tools to your sales success. Interestingly, however, most salespeople fail to employ them. And if you fail to employ them, it could prove fatal to your sale.

# Chapter 8

# Step 5: Convince Your Prospect of Your Claims

**Objective:** Convince—to provide powerful social, statistical, or third-party proof of your claims.

There is a basic fundamental truth in sales. People expect salespeople to make claims about their products or services. However, they are impressed when someone else does.

Once you've adequately presented your product or service, created great value for it, and ensured your presentation was 100 percent on target for your prospect, here's the next step.

**You say:** Now, let me show you what other people [or organizations] very much like you have to say about our _____ [product, service, company, warranty, delivery, etc.].

At this point, consider offering one or more of three ways for your prospect to experience corroboration of your claims.

For example, if your prospect shows concern or disbelief over quality or product issues you have claimed:

**You say:** Let me show you what _____, the leading trade journal in your industry, has to say about our quality.

113

or

**You say:** Let me show you how we rank in the latest research by *Consumer Reports* [or some other relevant, respected, third-party evaluation].

Put the hard copy of the report data directly in their hands. Let them read it for themselves. Then you follow up:

**You say:** You can see why we're so highly rated by those who research and rank [products/services] like ours, can't you?

If your prospect has shown concern over the credibility of your statements:

**You say:** Let me show you some letters we've received from some of the people we do business with, [people/companies] just like you.

At this point, show them letters from satisfied users of your product or service that you have prepared (highlighting key phrases, if possible) that help to corroborate your claims. Allow them to read, touch, and keep these letters. Then you follow up:

**You say:** Hopefully, you can see the reaction to what we provide. Do these comments satisfy any concern you may have relative to quality, delivery, service, price, etc.?

Three possibilities:

**You hear:** Yes, it does.

You've moved one step closer to the sale. In fact, you may want to take a closing action at this point (Step 6, Tie It Up).

or

**You hear:** No, not really.

or

**You hear:** I'm not sure.

If the prospect is dissatisfied, you should proceed to the next level:

**You say:** Would you like to speak to one of our [customers/ clients]? That way you can pose your question or have your concern answered personally by someone who clearly has nothing to gain. If that's what you'd prefer to do, here is a list of _____ [six is an ideal number] people who have agreed to talk with anyone like you who might have a question. Would you like to do that?

Two possibilities:

**You hear:** Yes, I would.

**You say:** That's good. Is there a person, or several people, on the list that you'd prefer to call? The reason I'm asking that is that I want to be sure to alert them to expect your call. We do this as a courtesy to them so that they can anticipate your call and be prepared for it. Is that OK with you?

**You hear:** That's fine.

**You say:** Do you have any idea when you might be calling them so that I can give them an idea as to the timing?

**You hear:** Within the next week or so.

**You say:** Good. Now, which one or ones do you prefer to call?

Once you've determined who will be called and when, you continue:

**You say:** You should have all of your calls completed by _____. Is that correct? Would you prefer that I call you a day or so after that, or should I wait for your call?

Get an answer. In either case, you need to be moving closer to finalizing the sale.

or

**You hear:** No, that's not necessary.

Two possibilities:

**You say:** OK, then, does everything look acceptable to you?

or

**You say:** What further evidence, if any, do you need to move ahead?

In either case, you're now forcing your prospect's hand. You'll determine if he or she is prepared to buy, is stalling, or needs more evidence.

We will consider the third possibility in a moment.

If it seems that the prospect is prepared to buy or is stalling, you need to move to finalize the sale. (Details on just how to do that are outlined in Step 6, Tie It Up.) Here's how you determine whether the prospect is prepared to buy or not.

**You say:** Why do you say that?

Two possibilities:

**You hear:** I'm ready to move ahead.

It's time to take a closing action at this point (Step 6, Tie It Up).

or

**You hear:** I would rather find out for myself.

**You say:** Would you like to experience the [product/service] yourself?

**You hear:** Yes, I would.

## Step 5: Convince Your Prospect of Your Claims

**You say:** We have lots of [customers/clients] who like to do that. When that's the case, we often run tests, trials, or beta tests. Let me tell you how that works.

Now, set up the test and determine what parameters will be used to define success. Once those parameters have been met, it's time for you to assume the sale.

## Get Satisfied Customers to Help You Sell

In the real world of selling, lots of clients will readily agree to have their name on a list to be contacted, if you ask them to do so. And how do you ask customers to indicate their level of satisfaction with your product or service?

Some people won't help you unless you ask them to do so. Those eager enough to do it on their own are few and far between. So to more fully and carefully prepare the tools you'll need to convince your prospects your claims are true, you'll need to know how to secure words of approval from your satisfied customers.

Let's talk about what to say, when to say it, and how to secure the testimonials you need. You'll need one or more of basically three types:

- Evidence of satisfaction, including a letter, audio, or video testimonial
- A name, contact information, and type of product or service provided, to be placed on a list agreeing to be called
- A willingness to supply you with the name and information you'll need to make contact with potential prospects

The exact time to approach someone about this is very easy to understand. It's when you have earned the right to do so. Period. However, there's one exception to that rule. When your customers say, "You're really great!" or something to that effect, you need to take advantage of that opportunity—even if you believe that you have more work to do to feel you have fully satisfied them. The real truth? They must be satisfied enough to say so. That's all.

**You hear:** I really like your _____.

**You say:** Could you put that in writing?

**You hear:** Of course.

**You say:** Would you like me to suggest some verbiage that you might use or would you prefer to phrase it in your exact words?

Two possibilities:

**You hear:** Yes, help me.

You then agree to help.

or

**You hear:** I'd prefer to use my own words.

In either case, you're in good shape. However, you're not done yet. You need to establish a specific time frame for receipt of the letter.

**You say:** How soon do you think I might expect the letter? I don't want to inconvenience you, but the sooner I can get it, the better!

**You hear:** When would you like it?

**You say:** I'd like it by _____. Is that acceptable?

**You hear:** That's fine.

or

**You hear:** No, but by _____ would be better.

Either way, you're fine. The goal? To get a letter indicating the customer's level of satisfaction with what you provided.

What should you do with the physical letter? Here are several suggestions:

- Make color copies of the original and use it in your sales presentation.
- Scan it for downloading as you need it and use it in either a digital or a hard copy format.
- Underline or highlight key words that reflect end results similar to what your prospect is trying to achieve. You can do this digitally or by hand.

You might also consider asking for a video or audio testimonial. These are powerful tools that can be deployed on a Web site, blog, or DVD.

**You say:** Would you be willing to allow us to record your thoughts about working with us and how our product has helped you?

**You hear:** Yes.

**You say:** When is the most convenient time for you to meet with us to record it?

Schedule a time that's convenient.

Another strategy is to have a prepared list of happy, satisfied customers whom prospects can contact if they choose to do so. Here's how to secure those who are most willing to be on the list.

**You say:** Would you mind if I placed your name, contact information, and type of [product/service] we provided to you on a list for other prospective customers to review?

Two possibilities:

**You hear:** Yes, that's OK with me.

**You say:** I will promise you this, if anyone does want to contact you, I will tell them that, as a matter of courtesy to you, I will inform you so you'll be able to anticipate their call. Does all of this sound OK?

**You hear:** That's fine.

**You say:** Good. I also promise that I'll only keep your name on the list for a short period of time. That way you won't have to worry about it. In fact, I'll even contact you when it's time for me to remove you from the list. What do you think?

or

**You hear:** No, I don't want to do that.

**You say:** I understand. However, is there any specific reason why you wouldn't be interested?

Based on the response, you may want to either resolve the concern or get your customer to agree to only a letter of recommendation. This is an opportunity to uncover any problems an otherwise happy customer may have.

If the initial response to your request is negative, you may also want to consider this approach:

**You say:** That's fine, I understand. However, if someone does want to talk with you, is that OK?

Then proceed accordingly.

Many prospects will ask for a list and never call anyone. They just want to be sure that you have a list of satisfied customers! However, in today's rapidly changing economic climate, reference checks have become far more important than ever before. What used to be an anomaly has become a regular and consistent practice.

When a prospect indicates that he or she will be contacting someone, you need to contact your customer and inform him or her that a prospect will be calling. Often, you can inform your customer of the possible call with an e-mail. However, if you choose to make a phone call, here's how that conversation usually goes:

**You say:** Hello, Terry. This is _____. How are you?

**You hear:** Hi, _____. How are you?

**You say:** I'm great. The reason for my call is that one of our prospective customers, Bob Jones with XYZ Corporation, indicated that he'd like to talk with you. Is that OK?

Here's the most interesting part. If you have placed highly satisfied prospects on the list, they will ask you this simple, straightforward question nearly 100 percent of the time:

**You hear:** What do you want me to say?

Your answer? Tell them to truthfully, of course, frame their response within the context of how you want to help your prospect address a need, handle a problem, or overcome an objective, or your prospect wants corroboration of your claims from an independent third party—your happy, satisfied customer. And your customers will do that, as long as you've earned the right for them to be totally, 100 percent enthusiastic about you, your product or service, and your organization.

## Overcome Objections in the Real World

It's a fundamental truth that highly successful salespeople don't encounter many objections. That's because they generally uncover the most likely objections in the Probe step with objection-testing questions, and then present their solution in a way that eliminates reasons for objections.

However, it's critical in a book of this type to cover at least the most common objections that salespeople will encounter no matter what product or service they sell. What are they?

- I want to think about it.
- I need to talk to _____ [my boss, spouse, partner, associate, attorney, accountant, advisor, etc.].
- Your price is too high.
- I don't see any reason to change [suppliers, vendors, etc.].

We'll deal with each one in a moment. However, first we need to deal with the specific dialogue that you'll need to use in order to transition into the exact formula for managing each.

Your prospect raises any of the four most common objections—or any of hundreds of others. (After all, it's the formula or pattern you'll need to master, not dealing with a specific objection.)

**You say:** I understand why you might say that. Is there anything else that causes you concern at this point?

Now, wait for an answer.

This response will do the following:

- It will neutralize any negativity.
- It will clearly show that you understand that your prospect might have a concern.
- It will uncover any other issue that may be causing your prospect to have an objection while isolating any specific objection(s).
- It will show that you really do want to know the reason(s) behind his or her response and deal with it.

Now, let's look at each objection and a specific response to each.

## FIRST COMMON OBJECTION

**You hear:** I want to think about it.

**You say:** I can understand why you might say that. Is there anything else that would cause you concern at this point?

**You hear:** No, not really. I just don't make decisions like this so quickly.

**You say:** I understand. What time frame would you like to have to think this over?

or

**You say:** I understand. What is it you'd like to think about?

or

**You say:** I understand. What is it you'd like to think about and what time frame would you like to have to think it over?

In each of these cases you are doing the following:

- You emphasize that you really do understand your prospect's concern.
- You give your prospect an opportunity to verbalize any other concern.
- You ask a question that will allow you to present your solution one more time.

For example:

**You say:** Let me emphasize that making a decision now certainly doesn't obligate you for the future. Let me explain.

or

**You say:** Let me stress that the time frame you select, will, of course, be one of your choosing. So, let me ask you this, what other information do you need?

## SECOND COMMON OBJECTION

Now, let's look at the second most common objection, "I need to talk to _____."

**You hear:** I need to talk to my accountant about this.

**You say:** I can understand that. Is there anything else other than talking to your accountant that concerns you at this point?

**You hear:** No, not really. But I do need to run this by him.

**You say:** If you don't mind my asking, what is it that you'd like to discuss with him?

You'll solicit the specific issue or question and either do your best to answer it for the prospect or offer to meet with the other person to help with this issue. Remember: You sell your product or service and can discuss it more effectively with the other person than your prospect ever could. However, you really should have discovered this objection earlier, shouldn't you?

## THIRD COMMON OBJECTION
How about the third most common objection, "Your price is too high"?

**You hear:** Your price is too high.

**You say:** I can understand why you might say that. Is there anything other than price that concerns you at this point?

**You hear:** No. It's just the price.

**You say:** If you don't mind my asking, what is it about the price that concerns you?

**You hear:** I just don't see any reason to spend that much money.

**You say:** Let me explain to you why our price is where it is.

You again recap the benefits the prospect will receive, how your product or service is superior, why your price is higher or, if it applies to your product or service, how you could remove certain components to meet the prospect's price demands.

## FOURTH COMMON OBJECTION
Finally, the fourth objection, "I don't see any reason to change."

**You hear:** I don't see any reason to change suppliers.

**You say:** I can understand why you might say that. Is there anything else that concerns you at this point?

**You hear:** No.

**You say:** If you don't mind my asking, if you could change, modify, alter, or improve anything at all about your current supplier, what would it be?

Your goal is to isolate this as the only objection (as you do in each and every case) and then determine if there's any single issue that's less than 100 percent, totally acceptable to the prospect with regard to the current supplier, vendor, or source.

## OTHER OBJECTIONS

In each example here, when you ask, "Is there anything else that causes you concern?" the response is "No." Unfortunately, in the real world, that may not be the case. Let's look at an example:

**You say:** Is there anything else that causes you concern?

**You hear:** Yes, there is.

**You say:** What is that?

**You hear:** I'm also concerned about the terms, warranty, and delivery schedule.

**You say:** Is there anything else that concerns you?

**You hear:** No.

**You say:** So, what I understand you to say is that the price, terms, warranty, and delivery are the only issues. Is that right?

**You hear:** Correct.

**You say:** Let's deal with each, if it's OK. Which would you like to deal with first?

**You hear:** The price.

Deal with the price issue first. Then ask your prospect which issue to deal with next. Be sure that you satisfy his or her concern with each issue, in order. Do this by asking, "Does this answer your question about _____?" When you're confident that you've dealt with each issue to your prospect's satisfaction, you're now prepared to move closer to finalizing the transaction.

The largest single issue relative to objections is to know that they should never arise. You should identify them either in pre-call planning through your internal advocate, in the Probe, or eliminate them in your presentation by circumventing them with a properly designed recommendation.

However, if objections come up, here's the formula for dealing with them:

1. Give your prospect verbal approval to have an objection.
2. Ask if there are other concerns.
3. Identify and isolate each issue.
4. Deal with each issue, one at a time, being sure that each is resolved before you move on to the next objection.
5. Don't be deterred from moving ahead with the sale.

Never forget that a "stall" simply means that your prospect wants to slow down the process, not feeling prepared to forge ahead with the sale, whereas objections are true issues that you need to resolve before you can move on with the sale.

# Chapter 9
## Step 6: Tie It Up—
## Finalizing Transactions

**Objective:** To empower your prospect to buy, solidifying the sale, servicing, and vertically integrating the new account.

In this step you ask the prospect to buy, negotiate an agreement, finalize, reinforce, and then cement the sale. You also service your new customer in ways that guarantee more sales, strong referrals, and an ongoing productive relationship.

Without securing a commitment, you won't have a sale, of course. And after all, isn't that your real purpose for being in front of the prospect?

However, it's important for you to understand that finalizing the transaction depends on everything you do in the first five steps. It begins with proper prospecting, positioning, and pre-call planning. But it doesn't stop there. You must also gain and secure trust with your prospect, ask the right questions, and make a strong and correct recommendation. You must also ensure your prospect believes your claims about your product or service and your organization, and trusts that both can help her achieve what she wants.

Now that you've gone through the first five steps successfully, it's crucial to know exactly what you should say to win the sale.

In spite of a strong temptation to provide you with a plethora of ways to finalize the sale, you need to understand, master, and apply one single powerful way to make a sale. It's far better to have one proven strategy and be able to use it correctly than it is to memorize a series of complicated maneuvers that, in the real world, you'll never use.

## The Assumptive Close

What is that one single powerful strategy? It's the assumptive close. It's called that because you are assuming that your prospect will buy and you're either making a straightforward statement or asking a simple question. And this close has been around for years.

Here are some examples of assumptive closes in the form of statements:

- Let me show you how we can get started.
- Let me send you a letter of agreement.
- Let's take care of the paperwork.
- I'll set you up for delivery on Tuesday.

Here are some assumptive closes in the form of questions:

- When would you like to get started?
- Can we go ahead and take care of the paperwork in order to get started?
- May I set delivery for Tuesday?

In each one of these cases, you imply that you assume your prospect will buy your product or service.

Again, however, in the real world, either of these methods will elicit one of three responses: "Yes," "No," or "I'm not sure." Now, let's take a look at how you would handle each of these responses.

**You say:** Let me show you how we can get started.

**You hear:** OK.

**You say:** Let's take care of the paperwork now and you can sign it. We can then get the order process set up.

You are now in business. Of course, in the real world you would use the specific verbiage related to your situation for handling the details of initiating the sale of your specific product or service (letter of agreement, purchase order, delivery schedule, etc.).

Another example:

**You say:** Would you like to get started?

**You hear:** Yes, let's go ahead.

**You say:** Good. Here's where we need your signature to get everything started.

However, you may not always receive such a positive response. If the response is negative, what do you do or say?

**You say:** Can we go ahead and take care of the paperwork to get started?

**You hear:** No, I don't think so.

**You say:** What is it that would cause you not to go ahead?

**You hear:** I need to discuss it with my wife.

**You say:** Is that your only concern, the only thing that would cause you not to go ahead with this?

Let's examine what just happened. You used the assumptive close only to discover that your assumption was incorrect! However, that's certainly not the end of the world.

Now you need to isolate your prospect's concern or objection ("What is it that would cause you not to go ahead?") and uncover any other reason ("Is that your only concern . . . ?").

Once you've isolated the problem and either identified

it as the only one or identified others, your next task is to try to resolve it to your prospect's satisfaction.

**You say:** If we can solve this issue to your satisfaction, can I presume that we will be able to go ahead?

You will hear either "yes" or "no." You then need to proceed accordingly. Here's how it works:

**You ask:** Now, what exactly, is your concern about _____?

**You hear:** I'm concerned about the warranty *or* I'm still concerned about spending that much money.

**You say:** As I understand it, if your concern about _____ can be resolved, everything else looks OK. Is that right?

**You hear:** Yes, I think so.

**You say:** I understand. Let's deal with your concern about _____.

You'll now work to resolve your prospect's concern by reapplying your solution in terms that resolve, solve, or eradicate the concern. During this process, be sure to ask course-correction questions consistently ("Does this answer your concern?" or "How does this look?" or "Does this look more acceptable?")

When you have resolved the concern(s) to your prospect's satisfaction, you'll again use some form of the assumptive close.

**You say:** If this solves your problem with _____, can we go ahead and get started?

or

**You say:** If this answers your concern, let's get started.

At this point, say absolutely nothing. Don't respond, utter a word, or say anything! Your prospect will either say "Yes," "No," or "I'm not sure." If the answer is "Yes," you've made a sale. If the answer is "No," you'll need to reapply the same formula as just described one more time. If the answer is "I'm not sure," you'll need to ask, "What is it that you're not sure about?" Then you'll deal—one more time—with the issue or concern and repeat the same process.

This is an important process to master. Never lose sight of the fact that if you're unable to deal with objections and finalize transactions you'll never be successful in sales. It's just that simple.

If you hear your prospect say, "I'm not sure" after you ask an assumptive question or issue an assumptive statement, you need to ask this question, "What is it that you're not sure about?" Whatever the prospect says, you'll need to respond with "I can understand that. What do we have to do to resolve that issue so that we can move ahead with this?"

Now, you can easily go ahead and resolve the issue(s) so that the sale can be won.

## Cement and Reinforce the Sale

Sales are won only when and if your prospect's check clears the bank! Never, ever believe that you can make a sale and then pack your bag and leave.

It's critical that you understand the mindset of most buyers, no matter what they've bought. Thoughts like these run through their minds:

- Did I do the right thing?
- Did I buy too much? Too little?
- How will I defend this to my boss?
- Did I pay too much?
- Should I have looked elsewhere?

Be sure to say things to cement and reinforce the sale:

**You say:** I'm sure glad that you decided to go ahead with _____. It's our best-performing model. You're going to like it.

or

**You say:** You'll feel confident knowing that you have the extended warranty. I'm glad that you decided to do that.

or

**You say:** You made the right choice. Congratulations!

**Remember:** You're reinforcing and cementing the sale to counter the thoughts of concern that can creep into your prospect's mind. Prospects generally don't verbalize these concerns, so you'll never know if they really feel like this. Simply assume that they feel like that and be sure to reinforce and cement the sale every single time.

## Follow Up the Sale

These strategies are essential to your success with your new customer on a long-term basis. Do you want to sell him or her more of your product or service? Do you want to use him or her as a referral source? If the answer to either of these questions is yes, then this is an important section for you to understand and master.

After you cement and reinforce the sale, you'll need to be very clear about what happens next. For example:

**You say:** I'll call you tomorrow to confirm that the delivery schedule has been finalized for next week.

or

**You say:** I'm going to go back to the office and make arrangements for Jane Green, our customer service manager, to contact you tomorrow morning.

or

**You say:** I'll be calling you no later than Thursday to reconfirm the details and guarantee proper shipment.

Bottom line? You must articulate some sort of action you're going to take, when you'll do it, and what that means to your new customer. Fail to do this at your own peril. Why? Because you need to start proving to your new customer, right now, that you're proactive, dependable, and capable of ensuring his or her satisfaction. Trust me: This will empower you significantly with your customers, and prove to them that you're interested in far more than collecting a commission, making a sale, or winning a contest.

Upselling your new customer at this point is much easier than you might think. After all, the tough part—the initial sale—is over, isn't it? That's often a good time to sell other products or services related to that sale. Upselling is happening all around us. Have you ever bought a dress and then the salesperson suggested shoes to go with that dress? How about a suit and you ended up buying a shirt and tie with it?

All you need to do is suggest an additional component or logical extension to your product or service. You might ask a question like this:

**You say:** Have you given some thought to adding the extended warranty?

You might make a statement and follow it with a question, like this:

**You say:** Most of our customers take advantage of the help desk option. Would you like to do that?

In any case, as counterintuitive as it may appear, upselling immediately after making a sale is far easier than waiting to do so later. Try it. You'll be surprised how easy it really is.

## FINAL THOUGHTS

These scenarios for the six steps of the sales process should provide you with the perfect phrases you need to prospect, seek appointments, meet prospects and customers, qualify prospects and ask questions, make effective presentations, prove your claims, create value, present price, finalize transactions, seek referrals, overcome objections, and service accounts. In Chapter 10, Advanced Selling, we'll get into some precise words, phrases, and strategies that work with specific types of prospects and customers.

# Part Three

## Additional Sales Scenarios: Four Types of Customers

# Chapter 10
## Advanced Selling

There are universal sales truths, principles, and concepts—and there are also some very precise words, phrases, and strategies that appeal to each specific type of prospect or customer. And that is very, very advanced selling.

This differentiation centers on a unique concept presented earlier in this book—a concept that most salespeople never understand, let alone master. Here it is:

**Prospects don't always buy what they need. They always, however, buy what they want.**

Here's the difference:

Needs are . . .

- Product-specific
- Rational
- Above the surface
- Based on fact

Wants, on the other hand, are . . .

- Product-neutral
- Emotional

- Below the surface
- Based on perception

As a consequence, here's the principle: For salespeople who can present their product or service (a need) in the way that their prospect wants to perceive it, a sale is much more likely.

Let's put it another way:

Prospects are more likely to buy what they need from salespeople who understand what they really want.

This final section will deal with how you can do this with four specific types of prospects:

- Entrepreneurs
- Corporate executives (not CEO)
- Purchasing managers
- Hospital administrators

These four were selected because they represent a cross section of prospect or customer types. Each was selected from our library of special reports that are available for order through our Web site, www.the wordsthatsell. com.

In every case, there are five specific wants that every prospect has, no matter what your product or service might be. Your job is to describe and position each of them before you actually present them. These are those five specific wants:

- **Primary Want:** The type of relationship that the prospect wants to have with a salesperson, supplier, or vendor.
- **Product or Service Want:** The way that the prospect wants to perceive the product or service he or she seeks.
- **Benefit Want:** The perception of the benefits that a prospect wants to receive in any product or service.

- **Provider Want:** The type of ideal provider that a prospect wants to do business with in securing a product or service.
- **Price Want:** How the prospect wants to perceive the ideal price.

What does all of this mean? That you need to properly position, describe, and articulate in absolute terms each of these wants (primary, product/service, benefit, provider, and price) to the prospect before you actually verbalize them in terms based on needs.

Specifically how you will do this is described in each special report included as part of this book. However, let's talk more about how this works. For example, to an entrepreneur the most important thing about any product or service is that it must be "practical, street-smart, and designed for their unique situation." And It makes no difference what the product or service might be! Here's an example of how you'd present your product or service to an entrepreneur:

"Before I get real specific about our service and how it works, let me first say that it's street-smart, practical, and designed for your unique situation. Now, let me describe it to you in detail . . . "

The purchasing manager wants to see any product or service as being "easy to understand, solid and safe, not technically challenging." So, how would you present your product or service to this type of prospect? Here it is:

"Before I get real specific about my product and how it works, let me first say that it's easy to understand, is a solid and safe purchase, and doesn't require a lot of technical education. Now, let me describe it to you in detail . . . "

Got the picture? Now, let's look at four specific prospects:

- Entrepreneurs
- Corporate executives who aren't CEOs
- Purchasing managers
- Hospital administrators

# Specific Words to Use When Selling to Entrepreneurs: Form a Special Instant Bond in Your First Interaction

## PRIMARY WANT

To form a strong bond with an entrepreneur, your presentation must begin with a description of what he or she really wants out of having a relationship with you. This specific bonding statement can replace the generic bonding statement outlined in Part Two.

To do this, you'll need to initially engage your prospect using phrases like the following:

- Being in charge
- Calling your own shots
- Personal independence
- Being your own person
- Making the business run your way
- Doing whatever you want to do, whenever you want to do it
- Having complete control over your business

## EXAMPLE OF A PRIMARY BONDING STATEMENT

- Independence, freedom, and calling your own shots are probably reasons you started your business in the first place. We know that. To see if we can help you achieve even more of that, do you mind if I ask you a few questions?

**WHY THESE WORDS WORK**

Surprisingly, most entrepreneurs aren't trying to build financial empires for themselves. Most of them went into business to achieve a far different goal: a steady, respectable paycheck without having to put up with a boss.

These prospects could never accept a position in a large organization, no matter how prestigious or well paying it might be. And if they ever do, they resent it and yearn to return to their entrepreneurial roots before too long.

If there's a fact about this type of prospect that rings most true, it's that they're virtually unemployable.

Why is that? Entrepreneurs generally resent any form of authority that's exerted over them. In fact, they lack the single characteristic every employee must have: being willing to obey the orders of a superior, even when they think the superior is wrong.

On top of that, entrepreneurs would never sit still for doing the things that employees are expected to do, like:

- Reporting their results
- Explaining their actions
- Justifying their decisions
- Appearing at times and places "on demand"
- Cooperating with a superior whose capabilities they believe aren't any greater than—and are probably inferior to—their own
- Accepting other people's decision-making authority

Being a cooperative employee runs against the very fiber of their being. As a result, their desire for personal independence—more than any other impulse—drives entrepreneurs to start their own businesses.

The impulse wasn't profit or riches. It was freedom.

That's an important distinction because it actually tells you the best way to approach this prospect, and—just as importantly—the approach you should avoid.

You can summarize almost all the approaches that most salespeople use with entrepreneurs in two words: profitability and growth. In other words, they promise either a better bottom line or a bigger business. A few promise both. And either or both are badly off target.

"Profitability" is nothing more than an intellectual abstraction for most entrepreneurs. They can't really "feel it." It has no emotional urgency, value, or meaning for them.

Of course, they'll always nod in agreement and make the right comments when the subject of profitability comes up. But it doesn't motivate them.

They relate more readily and eagerly to the amount of money they have in a checking account or the cash register at the end of every day, or week, or month.

Cash position has always mattered far more to entrepreneurs than profits ever could. It represents a reality they can easily understand and respect. When compared with the real-world significance of cash, profits seem empty and theoretical . . . merely an entry on a financial statement.

"Growth" raises the fear that they'll lose control over their businesses, a fear that comes from a perception that's fundamental to how entrepreneurs approach their businesses.

They fear that a major increase in the size of the business will outstrip their ability to manage it.

You need to understand that entrepreneurs rarely use any kind of coherent management strategy. They're more likely to manage in a very hands-on way. That's why they have difficulty handling managerial challenges that they can't handle both directly and personally.

If a decision has to be made regarding inventory control, for example, they have to "go and see for themselves" before deciding.

If their receivables department is having trouble collecting an overdue account? They'll say, "Give me the phone, I'll talk to 'em."

When they don't like the way the product is being shipped, they'll run down to the loading dock and show the people down there how to do it right, the way they did it when they were doing it themselves.

Managing a business is much more an act of physical labor than of intellectual insight for them. So, they manage by direct personal intervention rather than through memos, policies, or standards.

That, by the way, is one reason why they're so unwilling to delegate and why they do it so badly. Nothing of real importance is ever written down and passed on to employees so they can learn how to do their jobs satisfactorily. The result is a group of employees who are underinformed, undertrained, and undermotivated.

And of course, nobody in his or her right mind would delegate to people who are underinformed, undertrained, and undermotivated. The fact that the entrepreneur made those people that way always seems to escape his or her attention.

## Specific Words to Use When Selling to Entrepreneurs: Make Your Product or Service the Right Answer— No Matter What You Sell

### PRODUCT OR SERVICE WANT

To gain the best chance of having an entrepreneur believe and accept any product/service claim, you must carefully position your product or service before you start to describe it.

And you should position it by using words and phrases such as these:

- Designed specifically for your unique situation
- Practical
- Street-smart
- Nothing theoretical or abstract about it
- Won't put any demands on your time
- Won't strain your resources

### EXAMPLE OF A PRODUCT- OR SERVICE-POSITIONING STATEMENT

- Before we discuss our [product/service], let me stress that it's practical and street-smart. It's also been carefully designed for your unique business situation.

### WHY THESE WORDS WORK

Entrepreneurs are strongly attracted to products and services that they perceive have been designed specifically for their unique situations. If they had their "druthers," entrepreneurs wouldn't buy a single product or service that was not designed and developed precisely—100 percent—for their specific business, industry, application, or competitive environment.

During our research, we came across an entrepreneur in the St. Louis area who said, "I only buy from companies that do business on the Missouri side." He was referring, of course, to the Missouri side of the Mississippi River. According to him, companies "over on the Illinois side," as he put it, do business in a totally different way. Therefore, he couldn't possibly buy from a vendor who was unable to accommodate the difference between the two sides.

By the way, when asked for a specific definition of the difference between the two sides, he couldn't provide one. However, he was still fully convinced that there was a difference!

Entrepreneurs have that obsession because they don't like to make what I'll call a "conceptual leap." In other words, they don't eagerly make the move from the general to the specific, or from one application to another, or from one industry to another. And they usually resist adapting any broad, general concept to their own situation.

As a consequence, they're always suspicious that salespeople are trying to make them force a square peg into a round hole.

As a result, salespeople often hear entrepreneurs condemn their product or service by saying, "That doesn't apply to me" or "My business is different, it's unique." Actually, what they're really saying is "I'm unique, but you don't make me feel that way." Never forget: an entrepreneur and his or her business are practically the same.

Surprisingly, the actual words "specific to his or her unique situation" will even have different meanings for different entrepreneurs.

Those words are really a matter of perception. They might simply mean that your product or service was designed for an entrepreneurial type of business, or an owner-operated business, or a small business. If you pay close enough attention, the prospect will tell you which one he or she wants to hear.

When a product or service is perceived as "practical, street-smart, and not theoretical," most entrepreneurs believe that it will do all three of the following:

- It will eliminate complexity from their lives.
- It won't strain the company's resources.
- It won't put additional demands on their own personal time.

Entrepreneurs have no patience for complexity because it interferes with the hands-on, quick-action performance they consider so vital to their personal independence.

When things are too complex and ambiguous, the path is open for the abstract. Entrepreneurs don't trust anything abstract because it's theoretical rather than concrete. "Theoretical" just doesn't work in their world.

Anything that's theoretical is automatically "ivory tower," academic, or intellectual because it lacks the basic strength that comes from being "street-smart." It doesn't have any no-nonsense, hard-nosed practicality.

An entrepreneur draws a clear distinction between "the street" and the rest of the world. And only "the street" has the desirable virtue of being uncomplicated, down-to-earth, and easy to understand.

That's why entrepreneurs can be so frustratingly resistant to learning anything but hard information that deals with "how to." Anything that relates to "why" is of very little interest to them.

Their bias can be summarized in the statement: "Don't tell me why, just tell me how." Or "Don't tell me about the theory behind it, just tell me how to use it."

As far as entrepreneurs are concerned, stopping and thinking—which is what theory and ambiguity make them do—is a colossal waste of time. It gets in the way of "doing" and nothing must be allowed to stop that. Nothing must get in the way of action.

Entrepreneurs always seem to be running . . . from one fire to another, one crisis to another, and from one challenge to another. There's always a tension right below the surface when you talk with them.

What are they usually tense about? Burning through their resources.

It doesn't matter how rich in resources the business might be. They can't help but have either one of two perceptions about their resources: they're either completely insufficient or just barely adequate to do the job.

Earlier, we referred to the almost mystical relationship between entrepreneurs and their businesses. We said that owners and their businesses are practically one and the same. Therefore, an entrepreneur's idea of resources is personal—very, very personal.

If you listen carefully enough, you'll often hear them say

things like "I pay my bills." Although they mean that the business pays its bills, they can't stop themselves from speaking in the first person. "They owe me money" is synonymous with "They owe my company money."

And since resources often take on personal significance, they mean (over and above anything else) their own time.

This next statement is essential for you to understand. Even though the decision-maker might not ever get personally involved in the use of your product or service, it still must be perceived as not placing any additional demands on his or her time.

Nothing that passes in and out of the doors of that business is thought of in anything but the most personal of terms.

## Specific Words to Use When Selling to Entrepreneurs: Make Your Organization the Ideal Provider

**PROVIDER WANT**

To gain the best chance of having the entrepreneur accept your organization as an ideal provider, as with the other four wants, you must first position it before you start to describe it.

Describe your organization in the following ways:

- We're flexible.
- We're responsive.
- We're accommodating/willing to make accommodations.
- We never try to put a square peg in a round hole.
- We recognize your uniqueness.
- We're thorough.
- We follow through on everything.
- We cover all the bases for you.
- We're willing to do whatever it takes.
- We make sure every detail is covered.

**EXAMPLE OF A PROVIDER-POSITIONING STATEMENT**

- Let me tell you a little about our company. We pride ourselves on being flexible, responsible, accountable, and thorough. We follow through on everything. We cover all the bases, so you don't have to.

---

## WHY THESE WORDS WORK

An entrepreneur's desire for flexibility from you is a reflection of two other needs: personal independence and products/services that are designed specifically for his or her unique situation.

Small and medium-sized businesses outnumber giant companies by as much as 45-to-1. Yet, entrepreneurs perceive that almost every element of society favors large companies and institutions—university courses, professional and consulting services, taxes, trade shows, seminars, books, research data, legislation, health insurance, periodicals, and just about everything else that teaches, explains, or reveals anything that has any value. When they look at the structure of that world, they perceive a rigid, unyielding indifference.

The world is just too big and powerful for them to bend to their will, too impersonal to care about them, and too consumed by what's of no interest or value to them. It won't yield to their needs, or for that matter, even pay attention to them. And they resent that.

Therefore, they want to do business only with a provider who considers them important enough to warrant flexibility—or, if you will, very special treatment.

To be the ideal provider, you must be willing to make accommodations to what entrepreneurs consider their own unique requirements. Surprisingly, you won't have to actually be that flexible or even make that many exceptions. You simply have to be perceived as being willing to do so. And that's the secret! And essential for you to understand.

**Remember:** The need for personal independence is a

---

statement to the effect that "I'm different from all the others, so I should get unique treatment." They're not claiming to be better than everyone else, only different from them.

That overriding sense of uniqueness—of having special needs—is the main source of this type of prospect's highly suspicious attitude toward most people who sell them anything.

You may have noticed that they often begin the sales cycle with the assumption that the salesperson doesn't understand them and is "just trying to sell me something." And, as mentioned earlier, that's usually a square peg for a round hole.

Again, if entrepreneurs are going to perceive that your product or service was designed specifically for them, they also must perceive that you took all the necessary steps to make it the right way. That's why they always demand that you be more thorough and disciplined than they are. This is what might be called a "would have" or "should have" situation.

When they blame their chaos on the lack of resources—again, their most common complaint—they want to be assured that you did everything they would have done, if they had sufficient resources to make sure that your product or service is right for them. In other words, they would have done their own due diligence, allegedly, if they had the time and money to do it. That's the "would have" side.

On the "should have" side, a few entrepreneurs are honest enough to admit that their lack of discipline has nothing to do with resources. In those rare cases, they want to know that you did what they should have done.

Being thorough, therefore, means you'll protect them from either uncontrollable conditions ("what they would have done") or from themselves ("what they should have done"). In fact, the typical situation reflects some of both.

Although they are often short on resources, they're also notorious for not being thorough and they rarely follow through, even when ample resources are available.

That well-deserved reputation is a major contributor to their need for independence. As said before, they show a range of traits that really do make them virtually unemployable.

## Specific Words to Use When Selling to Entrepreneurs: Move Your Benefits to a Higher Level

### BENEFIT WANT

Like the other wants, in order to gain the best chance of having an entrepreneur believe and accept your benefit claims, you must first position them before you start to describe them.

Describe your benefits as delivering the following:

■ Order (in the business)
■ Control
■ Allowing you to be in control automatically
■ Order that reflects your personal wishes
■ No more chaos
■ An ability for you to never tolerate disorder again

### EXAMPLE OF A BENEFIT-POSITIONING STATEMENT

■ Our product/service will give you a lot more order and control. Any chaos will be reduced. That way you'll have a lot more automatic control without direct involvement on your part.

### WHY THESE WORDS WORK

If there's a word that reminds most entrepreneurs of their businesses, that word is "chaos."

Every senior executive in every large company must learn to deal with a certain amount of disorganization and tolerate it. Entrepreneurs, on the other hand, can't deal with it and can't tolerate it, either. Not a pretty picture, is it?

When they try to deal with chaos, they become victims of their own management style. If you recall, for them, running a business is an act of physical labor rather than one of intellectual insight, so they manage by direct, personal intervention.

Consequently, they experience an exhausting drain on their energies whenever they wear the manager's hat. Being in charge wears them down mentally; overcoming the disorder in the business is a challenge they'd do just about anything to avoid.

If they accept the challenge, they know they're going to be totally exhausted. But if they don't accept it, they have to tolerate it. And tolerating chaos is just as terrible an experience as trying to eliminate it.

Executives who aren't entrepreneurial view the companies where they work as their place of employment. Entrepreneurs, however, consider it practically their home, the place where their existence is on the line every day. It's where the drama of their lives is acted out from minute to minute.

Their fate ultimately rests on everything that happens within those walls. It's where their identity, value, and purpose are being tested constantly. And, as mentioned earlier, they consider themselves and the business to be almost the same entity.

The need entrepreneurs have for order is to believe that their lives aren't being squandered. After all, their business and life are one and the same. And they don't want to squander either one. However, because they deeply dread the challenges associated with their personal-intervention management style, they'd rather get control of the business in a different way—automatically.

They perceive that business problems are attributable to people—to themselves and their employees—which is why they tend to explain problems and failures in total human terms.

Since being in business is such an intensely personal experience for them, it's not surprising that successes and reverses are almost always seen as the result of human performance, good or bad.

Blind impersonal forces like marketplace dynamics might interest academics and other ivory-tower types, but they're just idle speculation to an entrepreneur. If a problem persists, people have to change the way they work in order to solve it. Period.

However, in starting their businesses, they made the statement that they have no interest in changing themselves. They are what they are and are stubbornly proud of it, even when they criticize themselves.

At the same time, they've grudgingly reached the conclusion that their employees won't change either or they don't know how to change their employees or they can't summon up the energy to make the effort.

One solution is to give the assignment to another person. But, when that happens, entrepreneurs immediately put themselves back in power as soon as the person makes a decision they don't like.

Because they could never surrender genuine control of the business to anyone else, except when they're ready to pass it to their hand-picked successors, order must come in some kind of automatic way, so that the owner doesn't have to intervene or change people's behavior. In effect, it just happens—and it happens the way the entrepreneur wants it to.

It doesn't take a great leap of logic to reach the point toward which all of the evidence leads: that entrepreneurs want their businesses to reflect their personal identities.

These prospects draw such personal value and identity from the business that it becomes an extension of themselves. It's as much a part of them as are their children. And, like all parents, they want their offspring to show something of themselves.

In no way is this an ego trip or anything as shallow as that. It's a matter of personal survival.

## Specific Words to Use When Selling to Entrepreneurs: Make Your Price, Rate, or Fee a True Bargain

**PRICE, RATE, OR FEE WANT**

One more time, as with the other wants, for the best chance of having the entrepreneur accept your price, rate, or fee, you must first position it before you ever quote it.

How you should position your price, rate, or fee before you present it:

- It costs the same as . . .
- It doesn't cost any more than . . .

**EXAMPLE OF A PRICE-, RATE-, OR FEE-POSITIONING STATEMENT**

- Before we discuss [price/rate/fee], let me stress that it won't cost any more than what you'd make from three additional sales. I'd also like to make sure you understand everything it includes . . .

**WHY THESE WORDS WORK**

Many types of prospects are likely to talk endlessly about things like cost-effectiveness, but the entrepreneur is one of the few who's really serious about it.

The reason for that is simple: no matter how large the business becomes, entrepreneurs always perceive that buying anything means taking the money out of their own pockets.

Earlier, it was indicated that running a company is an intensely personal experience for entrepreneurs.

Consequently, they consider the company's cash their personal money, just as they consider the furniture as being their furniture, the equipment as being their equipment, and so on.

They must perceive the ideal product or service as being worth the money and producing a tangible benefit on a virtual one-to-one basis for each dollar spent. And the best way to describe that is through graphic terms. In other words, choose a symbol that's familiar to your entrepreneurial prospect and use it as a model against which he or she can compare the price ("It costs the same as a set of tires"). For example, "Before I present our price, I'd like to make sure you understand everything it includes. The truth is that it will cost no more than three additional sales. Let me explain . . . "

## Specific Words to Use When Selling to Entrepreneurs: Letters and Advertising

### IN A LETTER OR E-MAIL

Dear _____,

**Form a Special, Instant Bond:** There's nothing like being your own person . . . doing whatever you want to do, whenever you want to do it.

**Make Your Product or Service the Right Answer:** To help you get there, a product or service has to be specific to your unique situation. It should also be practical and very street-smart.

**Make Your Organization the Ideal Provider:** But, even the best product or service won't do you much good unless it comes from people who are willing to do whatever it takes to make sure every detail is covered.

**Move Your Benefits to a Higher Level:** Then, you'll have control over your business that totally reflects your personal wishes.

**Make Your Price, Rate, or Fee a True Bargain:** And whatever you buy should never cost more than _____. [See the previous section on positioning your price, rate, or fee.]

I believe you'll find that [your product or service] and [company] can provide all of those things for you. But you, of course, should be free to make that decision for yourself.

[Now, state your purpose for writing the letter, what you want the prospect to do—a call to action—communicate your normal sales message, and finish the letter.]

## IN THE FORM OF ADVERTISING COPY
### Being Your Own Person

There's nothing like being your own person . . . doing whatever you want to do whenever you want to do it.

To help you get there, a product or service has to be specific to your unique situation. It should also be practical and very street-smart.

But, even the best product or service won't do you much good unless it comes from people who are willing to do whatever it takes to make sure every detail is covered.

Then, you'll have control over your business that totally reflects your personal wishes. And whatever you buy should never cost more than                    . [See the previous section on positioning your price, rate, or fee.]

I believe you'll find that [your product or service] and [company] can be all of that for you. But, you should be free to make that decision for yourself.

[Communicate your normal marketing message, state what you want the prospect to do—a call to action—and finish the ad.]

**Important:** Always put the Words That Sell in generic terms, as if you were describing "universal standards."

**Remember:** Their purpose is positioning. Once you communicate them, you can then use whatever words you normally use to tell the prospect about your product or service, your benefits, your company, and your price.

## Specific Words to Use When Selling to Entrepreneurs: Words That Don't Work

**Avoid** at all costs using these words and phrases to describe yourself, your organization, or your product or service.

However, feel free to use them to describe your competitors! Do so and you'll never have to criticize them in front of the prospect (which you should never, ever do in any circumstance anyway), if you know how to describe your competitors with the words that don't work:

- Organization
- Sophisticated
- Employee
- Theoretical
- Standardized
- Uniform
- The same for everyone
- Structured
- Procedures
- Growth
- Profitability

**EXAMPLE**

- XYZ is a sophisticated organization. Everything they do is based on a standardized format that comes from their highly structured research. What they do is the same for everyone. They accomplish this with procedures designed to help their customers have greater profitability. Their uniform approach appeals most to employees.

**WHY THESE WORDS DON'T WORK**

What do you think? It sounds like they're great—but not to this prospect! You'll notice that you're not saying one single negative word about your competitor. Of course, you don't want to say these things if they're not true. However, all of these words will work regardless of what you sell. Remember, though: use them with integrity.

# Specific Words to Use When Selling to Corporate Executives (Non-CEO): Form a Special Instant Bond in Your First Interaction

## PRIMARY WANT

To form a strong initial trust with this prospect, your presentation must begin with a description of what he or she really wants out of having a relationship with you. This specific bonding statement can replace the generic bonding statement outlined in Part Two when selling to a corporate executive.

In the Meet step you'll want to use words like these:

- Teamwork
- Not sticking your neck out
- Staying in the mainstream
- Sensible responsibilities
- Being involved in all of the important decisions
- Advancing steadily
- Protecting yourself from unwarranted intrusions
- Keeping everything on a safe course
- Insulating yourself

## EXAMPLE OF A PRIMARY BONDING STATEMENT

- Teamwork is critical to what you do and part of that is keeping you as involved as you want to be in making decisions. After all, advancing steadily is important. To see if we can help you achieve more of those things, do you mind if I ask you a few questions?

**Remember:** This can and will substitute for the generic bonding statement. However, this specific statement is good for use only with a corporate executive.

## WHY THESE WORDS WORK

The typical corporate executive wants to be thought of as a team player who is "comfortably anonymous" and never singled out for extraordinary responsibilities.

At the same time, he or she doesn't want to be left out of important processes and decisions, either. Sound contradictory? Not really.

Few corporate executives have the necessary ambition or critical political skills to keep advancing their careers carefully and purposefully to the very top of the pyramid, although some of them can come fairly close. As a result, they usually end their careers anywhere between middle management and a vice presidency or a directorship.

For corporate executives, therefore, the notion of teamwork and being a team player is vitally important. They have an inordinate need for "collective participation" because within the confines of the group is a comforting and protective anonymity, not from others within the company, but from the outside world.

It's revealing that CEOs and other high-ranking corporate officers are actually easier to reach on the phone than the typical corporate executive. This is because this breed of prospect has become an expert at hiding from the world inside the bureaucracy.

Becoming a vice-president or a director isn't, however, what we mean by "extraordinary responsibilities." Even though most corporate executives don't reach those levels, there's still nothing all that extraordinary about it.

An "extraordinary responsibility" would be taking on the task of contributing a significant improvement to the company's profit margin, achieving a dramatic turnaround of some sort, or developing an entirely new way of implementing a work process.

In other words, it's a challenge that is far out of the mainstream of normal corporate life . . . with a lot riding on the outcome. Even their careers. And corporate executives really don't want to have that much riding on what they do. At the same time, they don't want to be excluded from what they perceive to be "important processes and decisions."

Today, consensus is a crucial tool for CEOs. They won't move ahead with a decision until everyone who's involved has "signed off on it" or "had input into it." And among the people who have to sign off are the legions of corporate executives.

While they have an aversion to standing out in any exposed way—which is what an extraordinary responsibility will require—they're extremely sensitive to being left out of activities in which they believe they should be included.

In fact, given the consensus style of management practiced by virtually all CEOs, corporate executives have been conditioned to think in those terms. They expect to be included.

And if they're not, their world gets turned upside down and they become disoriented. It simply doesn't "feel right."

An interesting drama takes place when a corporate executive perceives that he or she has been omitted from an important decision-making process or project. Deviating from his or her usual cooperative, "don't rock the boat " style, the offended party can easily become the very obstacle with which you'll have to deal.

Corporate executives are not, in fact, above issuing threats that they will sabotage a project unless they are consulted on it, which certainly is exceptional behavior for someone who wants to be such a team player.

But that's exactly the point. Being excluded from the process shows that they are not "well-thought-of team players." And that is exactly what they don't want to happen.

The protocol that is part of their protective anonymity has been violated, and as a result, the familiar and comfortable way of doing things is stripped away.

Many corporate executives will instantly reverse themselves and become supportively cooperative at the very moment they're included in the process. And from then on, they'll often have so little to contribute to the actual decision-making process that you might wonder what all the fuss was about. The fuss, in fact, was not about wanting to insert exciting ideas into the process. It was really all about being included, as a good team player should be.

## Specific Words to Use When Selling to Corporate Executives (Non-CEO): Make Your Product or Service the Right Answer— No Matter What You Sell

### PRODUCT OR SERVICE WANT

As with all five wants, to gain the best chance of having a corporate executive believe and accept your product or service claims, you must precisely position it before you ever start to describe it.

Position your product or service by using phrases such as the following:

- Supports what you've already accomplished
- Is not a departure from what you are doing
- Right in line with the direction you are taking

### EXAMPLE OF A PRODUCT- OR SERVICE-POSITIONING STATEMENT

- Before I present our product/service let me stress that it really does support what you've already accomplished and isn't a departure at all from what you're already doing.

### WHY THESE WORDS WORK

If you approach a typical entrepreneur with a product or service that promises "more of the same," you're likely to be in for a major surprise. Independent business owners are known for making radical changes because they're forever struggling with the conditions that cause them to lose sleep every night. As a result, "more of the same"—or nothing more than a slight course correction—is rarely satisfying for the typical entrepreneur.

On the other hand, that slight course correction is about all the corporate executive can cope with.

When an entrepreneur admits to having wasted the company's resources on some form of foolishness, he or she doesn't have to fear the displeasure of a superior, because there isn't one. Entrepreneurs don't need, therefore, to be personally validated by every product and service they buy.

For senior executives, however, that's precisely the issue. It's the equivalent of professional suicide (that is, not being a highly regarded team player) to openly admit that their error in judgment has cost the company money, reputation, or whatever.

Radical shifts in direction are simply not a part of this prospect's universe, because shifts invalidate whatever the executive has worked so hard to sustain. Instead, every new purchase must be justified as one more complementary step, another building block that fits in neatly with all the previous steps and blocks.

Even in those rare situations in which a product or service represents a substantial departure from past practices, you'll find corporate executives concocting all sorts of elaborate reasons to prove that it's not really such a departure. In fact, their ability to torture reality sufficiently to satisfy this requirement is nothing short of awesome.

## Specific Words to Use When Selling to Corporate Executives (Non-CEO): Make Your Organization the Ideal Provider

### PROVIDER WANT

Again, to gain the best chance of having the corporate executive (non-CEO) accept your organization as an ideal provider, you must position it before you start to describe it.

Describe your organization in these terms:

- Team players
- Widely accepted
- Blend in well with everyone
- Committed to a team approach

### EXAMPLE OF A PROVIDER-POSITIONING STATEMENT

- Let me tell you a little about our company. We pride ourselves on being team players who blend in well with everyone. We operate under that total team concept, and as a consequence, are widely accepted within all of our customers'/clients' organizations.

### WHY THESE WORDS WORK

Your organization has to be acceptable to the corporate executive's superiors, peers, and subordinates.

Whenever you approach corporate executives, keep uppermost in your mind that you've been allowed to enter the "inner sanctum." That work environment is a highly private world into which few are allowed to encroach.

For example, salespeople often find that it takes months just to get an appointment with a corporate executive. Because of that, they make the mistake of concluding that he or she is a "tough sell" whose schedule is crammed with important meetings and other monumentally important events.

The opposite is almost always true.

It is shocking for most salespeople to learn that corporate executives actually fill their days with a bare minimum of critical work, instead spending excessive amounts of time to generate imperceptible results or no results at all.

During our research, to cite one example, we watched a corporate executive spend nearly an entire morning drafting a single three-page letter!

Their lunches are usually leisurely. Meetings are frequent, wordy, and unnecessarily long. Telephone conversations are often just as social as they are professional. Office banter and chitchat go on to a degree that would drive most entrepreneurs into an uncontrollable fury because they sign the paychecks and want nonstop work in return. But this is a totally different culture.

The reason these prospects can be so chronically and frustratingly inaccessible has nothing to do with their workloads. Instead, it has everything to do with their need for insulation.

The truth is that they're nervous about letting outsiders in and will do almost anything to avoid it. Every outsider, every provider they bring in is a reflection on themselves.

But there's a huge paradox here.

Corporate executives crave anonymity, which causes them to avoid making a large number of decisions. After all, the fewer decisions you make, the less chance both you and those decisions will stand out in any negative way.

Yet, because they make so few truly important decisions, each one they make takes on an exceptional significance, merely because it's such a rarity!

One such decision is the selection of a provider—you.

That's why salespeople who represent small and/or less well-known companies are so frequently disappointed when corporate executives decide to go with "old tried and true" providers with the big names and fabled reputations—the "least-risk vendor" scenario, even if their solutions are subpar, ineffectual, and overpriced. They appear to be safe and easily defensible. And that's one reason strong brands can breed poor sales skills!

And despite what you might believe, the decision had little to do with features, benefits, price, or any of the other conventional issues. It was, more often than not, strictly a matter of which provider would have the better chance of being the most acceptable to everyone who's involved.

And "everyone" implies a four-way perspective. Corporate executives are convinced that a provider must pass muster in "four directions":

1. Upward (with superiors)
2. To the right (with peers "on one side")
3. To the left (with peers "on the other side")
4. Downward (with subordinates)

Since the team concept is so fundamental to these prospects, an objection from any of the four directions can kill your potential sale—or put it squarely into the revenue stream of "old tried and true," again, no matter how expensive, overpriced, or ineffectual what you're selling might really be!

Another aspect of this four-way concern is the shifting loyalty most corporate executives have toward providers. These prospects can be boundlessly enthusiastic about doing business with you, only to instantly reverse their opinion if "flak" comes from any of the four directions.

For that matter, it's not even valid to use the word "loyalty," since the relationship most corporate executives have with their providers is better described as a "marriage of convenience." The relationship will only take on a tone of permanence if and when the provider establishes itself over a very long period of time. Until then, however, the provider is only as good as the latest opinion rendered by a superior, a peer, or a subordinate.

And that's only because that's how real, "dedicated team players" do it.

## Specific Words to Use When Selling to Corporate Executives (Non-CEO): Move Your Benefits to a Higher Level

**BENEFIT WANT**

Once more, to gain the best chance of having a corporate executive believe and accept your benefit claims, you must position those claims before you describe them to the corporate executive.

Describe your benefits as delivering the following:

- Nothing you have to defend or explain
- Nothing you have to apologize for
- Results everyone accepts
- The outcome everyone accepts

**EXAMPLE OF A BENEFIT-POSITIONING STATEMENT**

- Our product/service is nothing that you'll have to defend or explain. It will deliver the results and outcomes that everyone will accept.

**WHY THESE WORDS WORK**

Corporate executives are deathly afraid of being embarrassed in front of their coworkers and never want to be forced to defend an unpopular decision—or, worse yet, apologize for it. Any of those events could set their careers back for years or even derail them completely.

One of our salespeople even heard his prospect agree that a service he was selling was superior in every way to the one she had previously purchased. However, she had championed that decision and actually told him that if she recommended changing to the salesperson's service, it would be "career suicide." Needless to say, he never made the sale. And in fact, he didn't expect to, once he saw how totally consumed this buyer was with "career insurance," which in this case meant continuing to purchase an inferior service!

Given their insulation from the world outside their companies' doors, corporate executives have an unusual opinion of what the word "results" means. Unfortunately, it has little to do with the actual impact a company's product or service has on the customer.

Most prospects of this type are, surprisingly, emotionally and intellectually disassociated from that important aspect of the company's activities. They don't "feel" any genuine commitment, therefore, to such traditional notions as market share, customer satisfaction, "the bottom line," and so on. Oh, they can verbalize it with the best of them—but they don't really "feel" it. These concepts have an aura of unreality for them because their real world is insulated, defined by the boundaries of their departments and by the groups immediately surrounding them. They will, however, readily and fluently talk about "market share," "bottom line," "shareholder value," and all the rest. After all, using the right buzzwords makes them members of the team, doesn't it?

For them, the word which salespeople tend to use a bit too often—"results"—means that they could be embarrassed and/or forced to explain their decisions. Another bad word? "Accountability." In relation to you, both mean the buying decision. And, although accountability really is a watchword in business today, it is far more a word to use than an action to take or a process to implement.

There is an old saying: "Victory has a thousand fathers; defeat is an orphan."

With amazing skill and dexterity, corporate executives will widely distance themselves from an embarrassing decision—even if they are the ones who made it! In their environment, no one can afford to take that kind of heat.

# Specific Words to Use When Selling to Corporate Executives (Non-CEO): Make Your Price, Rate, or Fee a True Bargain

## PRICE, RATE, OR FEE WANT

As with all wants, to gain the best chance of having a corporate executive accept your price, rate, or fee, you must first position it before you start to quote it.

How should you position your price before you present it to this prospect?

- Priced within the mainstream
- In line with the industry

## EXAMPLE OF A PRICE-, RATE-, OR FEE-POSITIONING STATEMENT

- Before I give you the exact [price/rate/fee], let me stress that it's absolutely in line with the industry and is certainly priced within the mainstream. I'd also like to be sure that you know everything it includes . . .

## WHY THESE WORDS WORK

Your price, rate, or fee must be perceived as being close to that of your competition.

And with this prospect, pricing your product or service substantially higher than your competition's is a recipe for disaster.

Not even the most courageous corporate executive—not even the one who is completely enchanted with you—will be able to comfortably pay what others could perceive as an inflated price in their world.

You must understand, however, that the reason has nothing to do with saving their employer money, because there is little motivation among these decision-makers for that sort of thing. A budget is, after all, just a budget. It's not their money. Although they can be depended on to say all the right things about cost savings and so on, that's just so many words.

In their world, not paying an inflated price, rate, or fee is strictly a matter of the personal credibility of a team player.

# Specific Words to Use When Selling to Corporate Executives (Non-CEO): Letters and Advertising

## IN A LETTER OR E-MAIL
Dear _____,

**Form a Special, Instant Bond:** You should be able to stay in the mainstream—with sensible responsibilities—while being involved in all of the important decisions, as you keep everything on a safe course.

**Make Your Product or Service the Right Answer:** That requires products and services to support what you've already accomplished because they are right in line with the direction you are taking.

**Make Your Organization the Ideal Provider:** It also requires good team players who are widely accepted for blending in well with everyone.

**Move Your Benefits to a Higher Level:** When you get that, there's nothing you have to defend or apologize for because the results are what everyone expects.

**Make Your Price, Rate, or Fee a True Bargain:** On top of that, they expect a price, rate, or fee in line with the industry.

I like to think that [your product or service] and [company] can provide all of those things for you. But you, of course, should be free to make that decision for yourself.

[Now, state your purpose for writing the letter, what you want the prospect to do—a call to action—communicate your normal sales message, and finish the letter.]

## IN THE FORM OF ADVERTISING COPY
### Staying in the Mainstream

You should be able to stay in the mainstream—with sensible responsibilities—while being involved in all of the important decisions, as you keep everything on a safe course.

That requires products and services to support what you've already accomplished because they're right in line with the direction you're taking.

It also requires good team players who are widely accepted for blending in well with everyone.

When you get that, there's nothing you have to defend or apologize for because the results are what everyone expects.

On top of that, they expect a price, rate, or fee that's in line with the industry.

We like to think that [your product or service] and [company] can both be all of that for you. But, you should be free to make that decision for yourself.

[Communicate your normal marketing message, state what you want the prospect to do—a call to action—and finish the ad.]

**Important:** Always put the Words That Sell in generic terms, as if you were describing "universal standards."

**Remember:** Their purpose is positioning. Once you communicate them, you can use whatever words you normally use to tell the prospect about your product or service, your benefits, your organization, and your price.

## Specific Words to Use When Selling to Corporate Executives (Non-CEO): Words That Don't Work

Avoid at all costs using these words and phrases to describe yourself, your company, or your product or service.

However, feel free to use them to describe your competitors! Do so and you'll never have to criticize them in front of the prospect (which you should never, ever do in any circumstance anyway), if you know how to describe your competitors with the Words That Don't Work:

- Accountability
- Plot an unusual course
- Considerable responsibilities
- Keep your door open to everyone
- Be out in front
- Lead the pack
- A departure
- Shift direction
- Change from the ground up
- Substantial change
- Defend
- Explain
- Surprising results
- Unexpected

### EXAMPLE

- XYZ is a great organization. They're very good at introducing change from the ground floor up. They like to help people like you get out in front and plot unusual courses. There's a lot of accountability related to what they do.

**Remember:** Don't say things that aren't true! However, if these words do, in fact, express what your competitor does, describe them in this way.

# Specific Words to Use When Selling to Purchasing Managers: Form a Special Instant Bond in Your First Interaction

## PRIMARY WANT

To form a strong bond with this prospect, your presentation must begin with a description of what he or she really wants out of having a relationship with you. When selling to a purchasing manager, this specific bonding statement can replace the generic bonding statement outlined in Part Two.

Initially engage your prospect using phrases like these:

- Getting recognition
- Being respected for what you do
- Getting credit
- You probably do a lot more than you get credit for
- Gaining respect
- You're doing important work
- Making a big contribution
- You're important to your company's success

## EXAMPLE OF A SPECIFIC PRIMARY BONDING STATEMENT

- You make significant contributions with the difficult decisions you make. And that's important work. To be sure that we can help you continue to do that, do you mind if I ask you a few questions?

**Remember:** You'll have first issued your statement of intention by saying, "My purpose is to have a chance to meet you and ask you a few questions."

**WHY THESE WORDS WORK**

The typical purchasing manager wants to be considered by senior management as being equal to the company's "line" personnel, and to receive the same kind of respect, recognition, and validation that those people garner (and that the purchasing manager doesn't believe that he or she is receiving).

Never forget: These prospects are "staff," a status that differentiates them from their coworkers in the "line" divisions and departments.

The dominant bias in most companies is that line people are more important than staff people because line people are supposedly "the best and the brightest."

In a manufacturing firm, for example, the line divisions are sales and manufacturing (or production). They're considered "line to the product" because one of them builds it and the other sells it.

All of the other divisions and departments—purchasing, human resources, and so on—are "staff" because they support and service the line divisions/departments.

Due to this bias, purchasing managers are sometimes resented because:

- They supposedly work safely "behind the lines," where they're insulated from the dangers "in the trenches."
- They're considered only marginally important.
- They're not thought of as competent.
- They don't get credit for making a significant contribution to the company's success.

As a result, most of them have very little influence with their user departments.

Salespeople often have the frustrating experience of getting purchasing managers excited about their product or service, only to have the actual user fail to even show up for a meeting to discuss it! Has that happened to you? It has certainly happened to us—more than once!

Purchasing managers know that that bias is lurking beneath almost every contact they have with the line divisions. In response, they either strive to overcome it or retreat behind a wall of self-protective defensiveness. And since defensiveness is more typical, it's not unusual for you to find them becoming "territorial."

Given this lack of support and confidence from varied user groups, purchasing managers are often put in the role of the "go-between." They essentially "run back and forth" between the user group and the salesperson, trying to please the former and driving the latter to distraction.

As a consequence, they can be frustrating for you to deal with because even their own user departments usually fail to deal with them properly. So, they're often unsure about what to buy or the conditions under which to buy it.

Users rarely take the time to inform purchasing managers of anything but the most rudimentary facts around what they need. And users generally transfer any buying authority to the purchasing department on issues of no perceived importance.

"If it meets the specs, I don't care who you buy it from," is a comment purchasing managers report hearing frequently from their users. It communicates a lot between the lines because another way to say it is "I made the important decision. Now, you can make the unimportant one."

It's not unusual for salespeople to perceive purchasing managers as being excessively demanding or even unreasonable. Specifically, salespeople often claim that many purchasing managers are so obsessed with price that they seem to place little weight on quality or value.

Many purchasing managers are known for their almost single-minded focus on price. However, it's quite often just a misperception that purchasing managers are ordered to buy at the lowest available price. There is ample evidence to prove that something else is going on.

Here are some research results. Over 62 percent of the purchasing managers studied in so-called "lowest-price" environments admitted to legally adjusting their specifications/calculations to award a favored provider whose price wasn't the lowest. In another study, on-time delivery superseded price as the major buying criteria.

Other typical reasons for purchase have to do with issues such as useful product life, anticipated benefits, compatibility, upgrade ability, and a number of other factors that could "fudge" the issue of price.

When asked what makes a provider "favored," the factors that appeared again and again were "sincerity," "making the purchasing manager feel respectable and important," "a lack of technical obsession," and "patience."

On the other hand, when purchasing managers don't perceive a salesperson as being that way, these prospects can become rigidly demanding on such issues as price and delivery. They might also conduct quite rigorous facility inspections and use some sort of supplier equipment checklist as a fierce measuring stick.

In other words, if you can't satisfy the purchasing managers' need for importance, they're going to create their own satisfaction by becoming "tough" buyers. And that's your fault!

## Specific Words to Use When Selling to Purchasing Managers: Make Your Product or Service the Right Answer— No Matter What You Sell

### PRODUCT OR SERVICE WANT

Like with all prospects, to gain the best chance of having a purchasing manager believe and accept your product or service claims, you must position them before you start to describe them.

Position your product or service with these phrases:

- Easy to understand
- A solid and safe purchase
- Doesn't require a lot of technical education
- Not technically challenging

### EXAMPLE OF A PRODUCT- OR SERVICE-POSITIONING STATEMENT

- Before I present our [product/service], let me stress that it's easy to understand, isn't technically challenging, and certainly represents a solid and safe purchase.

### WHY THESE WORDS WORK

These prospects frequently feel vulnerable and highly self-conscious, as words such as "sincere" and "patient" demonstrate.

And much of what they both want and fear has to do with their being "nontechnical."

That means that, despite whatever knowledge they might have of technical products and services, they can't really understand all the particular ones they're buying.

For example, a purchasing manager might know a lot about how microprocessors are manufactured, which is an obviously technical application. Yet, she might be assigned to purchase narrow pipe components (that is, tube connectors) and know nothing about them. So she is "technical" when it comes to buying microprocessors but very "nontechnical" when she has to buy narrow pipe components.

Of course, it's usually more common for purchasing managers to understand a little about PC boards and components, but not enough to qualify as technical experts.

However, they're in a position of power—because they can issue purchase orders—even though they're definitely "nontechnical." It's crucial, therefore, that purchasing managers perceive any product or service they buy as being "easy to understand."

However, even if your product or service is, in reality, easy to understand, don't assume that you have no challenge here. What your product or service actually is has little to do with how it's perceived.

Keep this in mind: When perception and reality conflict, perception always wins—and it wins hands down, every single time. Far too many salespeople make the mistake of assuming that the realities associated with their products and services will automatically match the decision-maker's perceptions. That is rarely the case.

Not only are most purchasing managers branded with the label of "nontechnical," they're also well aware of it . . . and they resent it.

But to be completely candid about it, only the rarest purchasing managers make a strong effort to correct the situation.

The typical purchasing manager has amazingly little desire to learn everything he or she can about the products and services to be purchased. In fact, purchasing managers actually resist most attempts to educate them beyond the most basic levels.

One of the reasons for the resistance is the reality that the purchasing profession has undergone a dramatic change over the past few decades.

There was a time when most purchasing managers considered purchasing to be their careers. They studied it, studied the products and services they were supposed to buy, and acted in every other way as a professional usually does.

However, 10 to 15 years ago, the balance shifted from the traditional purchasing manager to a more "modern" type—those who consider the position to be nothing more than a "résumé stop" on the way to something better.

The real fact is that today's average purchasing manager doesn't have nearly the same depth of intellectual curiosity or technical knowledge his or her predecessor had decades ago.

Another common reason for the general resistance among purchasing managers toward education is just plain emotional fatigue. They're tired of seeing themselves struggling behind the knowledge curve, which is exactly their reaction when you take a stab at educating them.

In the old way of selling, the salesperson buried the prospect under an avalanche of whatever "techno speak" was common to the application. Buzzwords and dense jargon flew around in a confusing swarm that left this prospect with the depressing belief: "I won't ever be able to learn this stuff."

On top of that, the only time most salespeople even made an attempt at education was when they were desperate. They sensed that the sale was slipping away—or the purchasing managers might have told them outright that it was "no sale"—and they reacted by verbally assaulting the prospect with all sorts of technical information about their product or service.

In the typical scenario, the purchasing manager was using price as the excuse for not buying and the salesperson responded with a torrent that followed this logic: "We charge more than our competitors because . . . [techno speak]."

This, of course, was the last thing this type of prospect wanted to hear, and as a consequence, didn't pay attention anyway. But even today, purchasing managers, like all other prospect types, use price as an excuse—not always, but usually—for not buying.

By the way, don't be misled by the term "techno speak." You could be selling anything from computer programming services to pencils and there will always be some "techno speak" (sometimes called jargon) in your industry.

So, the "education" a purchasing manager got from a typical salesperson was really a relentless browbeating, a desperate and self-interested reaction to a missed sales opportunity.

However, even today for this prospect, the ideal product or service would be so simple that it would require no education whatsoever, technical or otherwise. And if your product or service fits that mold, you're automatically way ahead of the game.

But if it doesn't, you must face the challenge head-on. And, except for the very simplest products and services, a certain degree of education is unavoidable. Purchasing managers know it and accept it.

Make certain at least, that purchasing managers perceive your product or service as not overly technically challenging or requiring significant education. Even if you have the world's most complex product or service, your prospect must perceive it otherwise. Creating that perception will make whatever education is required easier for you to deliver and for the purchasing manager to accept.

# Specific Words to Use When Selling to Purchasing Managers: Make Your Organization the Ideal Provider

## PROVIDER WANT

To gain the best chance of having a purchasing manager accept your organization as an ideal provider, you must position it, too, before you start to describe it.

You need to position your organization with these words:

- Sincere
- Nonjudgmental
- Patient
- Not technically obsessed with your product or service
- More interested in your customers than in what you're selling
- Attach no strings to relationships with purchasing managers
- People

## EXAMPLE OF A PROVIDER-POSITIONING STATEMENT

- Let me tell you a bit about our company. We pride ourselves in being patient, not technically obsessed with what we sell, and far more interested in our customers than in what we sell.

## WHY THESE WORDS WORK

For reasons that are both real and perceived, purchasing managers consider most salespeople as being less than sincere. Much of that perception has been formed historically as a result of the tactics used by salespeople, some of which have been identified in this book.

The purchasing manager's desire for sincerity is, in fact, a reflection of his or her feeling of vulnerability and the fear that he or she really isn't up to the task.

Remember: most prospects who deal from any position of strength rarely worry about how sincere you are.

However, that's an advantage most purchasing managers don't usually have. And because they often "don't really know what they're buying," they have nothing much to rely on but a salesperson's sincerity.

Purchasing managers perceive most suppliers as "conditional" in that the provider's interest in them varies according to the situation, thus putting conditions on the relationship. In other words, the provider demonstrates interest only when there's a sale to be made.

This purchasing manager needs to believe that you see him or her as being more important and valuable to you than simply being a "buying machine." The purchasing manager can't think of your interest in him or her as being based solely upon a sale being made.

You must also be nonjudgmental. Here you have prospects who already feel judged enough by the people they work with. And they certainly don't want or need another person in their lives who seems judgmental.

Other parts of this chapter have addressed the issue of the decision-maker being "nontechnical." And if we seem to be hammering away at it, please forgive us. It happens to be a crucial issue, one that affects every aspect of your relationship with purchasing managers.

Be careful that you're not perceived as being technically obsessed with your product or service, even if that product or service is easy to understand and capable of being bought safely without much technical education.

You already know that being "nontechnical" is a badge of dishonor for most purchasing managers, a source of their "corporate inferiority complex."

That diminished self-perception stems in part from their realization that they're "staff." According to many of their coworkers, that makes them somehow less important than the people in "line" departments.

That bias is reinforced even further by the reality that purchasing managers are considered "nontechnical."

And no one in any technical environment—not user groups, no one—ever uses that expression in anything but the most derisive and disapproving tones.

As if they don't hear enough of it from inside their companies, purchasing managers are also reminded of it by their suppliers. Of course, the supplier never makes an open issue out of it, but the perception comes across loud and clear.

As I said before, the typical provider can't resist the urge to "educate" purchasing managers about the esoteric complexities of their product or service, which they rarely do for the decision-maker's benefit.

Salespeople resort to the "education tactic" whenever they sense a wall of resistance over issues like price, delivery, and so on. By trumpeting the technical virtues of whatever they're selling, they hope to overcome any problems with regard to those other issues. And it just doesn't work.

Worse yet, it aggravates the prospect's deep sense of inferiority and intensifies his or her resistance to making a buying decision that's going to please the provider.

Therefore, you must avoid creating the impression of being "technically obsessed."

Being exposed to providers who, in the words of a purchasing manager, "are in love with their own products" makes the nontechnical purchasing manager extremely uncomfortable.

A provider speaks a language the decision-maker can't even understand, is enchanted with things of no interest to the decision-maker, and shows impatience when the decision-maker "doesn't get it."

Your patience with the purchasing manager is another vital ingredient in the relationship. It's related to everything I've said up to this point about his or her being nontechnical and uninterested in a thorough education about a product, service, or supplier.

Most purchasing managers want some education, if for no other reason than that it's simply unavoidable. However, it has to occur under specific conditions, according to certain guidelines:

1. **Simple terms**—The education must be expressed in simple and easy-to-grasp terms, but not be so rudimentary as to be insulting. You must strike a very delicate balance in this regard.
2. **Not related to sales**—You should never offer the education when you're trying to make or save a sale. In other words, it can't be perceived as an attempt to use technical information the way most providers use it.
3. **Gradual**—The education must be delivered in small "packets" over an extended span of time. And if you're in

doubt, err on the side of making the packet smaller and making the time span longer.

4. **Minimal**—Don't be overly ambitious. These prospects have no desire to be technical wizards. They simply want and need to know enough so they can avoid embarrassing themselves with glaring mistakes.

Always refer to your organization as "people." That one, single word could turn out to be one of the most important of all. It's important for you to "personalize" yourself and your organization for these prospects. You'll score a major positioning victory if you can create the perception that you're actually a group of people and your competitors are merely companies or organizations.

Almost anything that's de-personalized makes the purchasing manager feel uncomfortable. People, on the other hand, are something he or she can easily understand.

## Specific Words to Use When Selling to Purchasing Managers: Move Your Benefits to a Higher Level

### BENEFIT WANT

To gain the best chance of having a purchasing manager believe and accept your benefit claims, you must position them before you start to describe them.

Describe your product or service as delivering the following benefits:

- Things that should run smoothly for you
- Quietly
- No crises
- Decisions that are certain and sure

### EXAMPLE OF A BENEFIT-POSITIONING STATEMENT

- Our product/service will allow things to run smoothly for you. I guarantee that you can make decisions that are certain and sure.

### WHY THESE WORDS WORK

It's far more common for this type of prospect to be recognized for poor performance rather than good.

In today's selling environment, the corporate self-preservation game of assigning blame to anyone but oneself means user departments have mastered the tactic of shifting all of the accountability for mistakes to the purchasing manager quite well.

So for example, when a provider doesn't deliver on time, it was the purchasing manager who selected them. A bad purchase is never hung on the user's door. It's always dropped right at the feet of the purchasing department.

Underlying this almost exclusive concentration on negative recognition is the corporate bias we mentioned before.

If you start with the assumption that the purchasing manager does "no-brainer" glorified clerical work, two unfavorable conclusions automatically fall into place:

1. Performing a mindless task well doesn't deserve praise because no extraordinary effort or talent is required.
2. Mistakes are practically unforgivable because the supposedly unchallenging nature of their work puts human error beyond the realm of acceptability.

In other words, success will go unnoticed while mistakes draw an unbelievable amount of fire.

One of the responses you hear most often when speaking with purchasing managers is the desire to "avoid making mistakes."

They need a tremendous amount of decision-making certainty. That means that making the right decision ensures satisfying the user group. But make sure you understand what that means.

Unfortunately, purchasing managers take much of their personal value from the user group's satisfaction with their performance. Unfortunately, that sense of satisfaction is almost never expressed, unless you define "expressed" as the absence of complaining.

Don't, for a single moment, believe that you can reverse a trend that has existed for decades. In other words, your product or service won't cause user groups to suddenly begin heaping praise on the purchasing department.

But what you can hope for—and what the purchasing manager is willing to settle for—are "quiet" working conditions. Given the pressures these prospects are subjected to, it's understandable that they want quiet working conditions. But this need has an even deeper significance than that.

To someone who's accustomed to hearing complaints, silence from the user department is the equivalent of approval. It may not be the ideal reaction, but it's better than what they're used to hearing.

## Specific Words to Use When Selling to Purchasing Managers: Make Your Price, Rate, or Fee a True Bargain

### PRICE, RATE, OR FEE WANT

To gain the best chance of having a purchasing manager accept your price, rate, or fee, you must position it before you start to describe it.

Here's how you should position your price, rate, or fee before you present it:

- Directly related to the benefits you'll receive
- Justified by the benefits
- Easily translated into the benefits you get

### EXAMPLE OF A PRICE-, RATE-, OR FEE-POSITIONING STATEMENT

- As I give you my [price/rate/fee], please bear in mind that it's directly related to the benefits you'll receive. In fact, it will be more than justified by those benefits. I'd also like to make sure that you understand everything it includes . . .

### WHY THESE WORDS WORK

Of all the prospect types, purchasing managers probably have the most notorious reputation for price sensitivity.

In reality, they personally care very little about how much you charge for your product or service. It matters only when it becomes a cause of controversy between or among themselves, their superiors, and/or the finance department.

If you recall from the case study mentioned earlier, purchasing managers will often actually go out of their way to do business with the providers they favor. But that's possible only when your price, rate, or fee—if it's higher than what your competitors are charging—can be translated into benefits. In other words, the purchasing manager has to be able to say, "Even though they charge more, I still chose them because . . . "

## Specific Words to Use When Selling to Purchasing Managers: Letters and Advertising

**IN A LETTER OR E-MAIL**

Dear _____,

**Form a Special, Instant Bond:** You should get respect for what you do, and you probably do a lot more than you get credit for—important work that makes a big contribution to your company's success.

**Make Your Product or Service the Right Answer:** You can improve that situation with products and services that are safe purchases because they're easy to understand and don't require a lot of technical education.

**Make Your Organization the Ideal Provider:** It takes special people to come out with a product or service like that, people who are more interested in the customer than in what they're selling.

**Move Your Benefits to a Higher Level:** With teammates like that, things will run smoothly for you—quietly, with no crises.

**Make Your Price, Rate, or Fee a True Bargain:** Then, the price, rate, or fee can be easily translated into the benefits you get.

I like to think that [your product or service] and [company] can provide all of those things for you. But you, of course, should be free to make that decision for yourself.

[Now, state your purpose for writing the letter, what you want the prospect to do—a call to action—communicate your normal sales message, and finish the letter.]

## IN THE FORM OF ADVERTISING COPY
### You're Doing Important Work

You should get respect for what you do, and you probably do a lot more than you get credit for—important work that makes a big contribution to your company's success.

You can improve that situation with products and services that are safe purchases because they're easy to understand and don't require a lot of technical education.

It takes special people to come out with a product or service like that, people who are more interested in the customer than in what they're selling.

With teammates like that, things will run smoothly for you—quietly, with no crises.

Then, the price can be easily translated into the benefits you get.

We like to think that [your product or service] and [company] itself can be all of that for you. But you, of course, should be free to make that decision for yourself.

[Communicate your normal marketing message, state what you want the prospect to do—a call to action—and finish the ad.]

**Important:** Always put the Words That Sell in generic terms, as if you were describing "universal standards."

**Remember:** Their purpose is positioning. Once you communicate them, you can then use whatever words you normally use to tell the prospect about your product or service, your benefits, your organization, and your price.

## Specific Words to Use When Selling to Purchasing Managers: Words That Don't Work

Avoid at all costs using these words and phrases to describe yourself, your organization, or your product or service.

However, feel free to use them to describe your competitors! Do so and you'll never have to criticize them in front of the prospect (which you should never, ever do in any circumstance anyway), if you know how to describe your competitors with the words that don't work:

- Challenging
- Highly technical
- Technology
- Technological
- Complex
- Make a judgment
- Education
- No brainer
- Conditional
- Systematology
- Non-Interactive
- Independent
- Requires study

### EXAMPLE

- XYZ has a very technical product. It requires a lot of education to fully understand it. It's somewhat complex. Therefore, purchasing it requires study.

**WHY THESE WORDS DON'T WORK**

You're not saying anything bad about your competition by saying this. However, you are describing them in words that aren't strong, positive words to this prospect.

However, remember not to use these words or phrases loosely, carelessly, or without regard for the facts. Don't use them if they're not true. Always sell with integrity.

## Specific Words to Use When Selling to Hospital Administrators: Form a Special Instant Bond in Your First Interaction

### PRIMARY WANT

To form a strong bond with a hospital administrator, your presentation should include a description of what you believe he or she really wants out of having a relationship with you. This specific bonding statement can replace the generic bonding statement outlined in Part Two.

To do this, you'll need to initially engage your prospect using phrases like the following:

- Hospitals that run the best are the ones where the administrator is in control
- Stay in control
- Get results that impress the people who are watching
- The world pays attention to people who get results
- Take control and keep It
- Put control and authority where they belong
- Move in the direction you want to go
- Climb the next step up the ladder

### EXAMPLE OF A SPECIFIC PRIMARY BONDING STATEMENT

- Because hospitals that run the best are the ones where the administrator is in control, that's how we'd like to work with you. To help you get results that impress the people who are watching, do you mind if I ask you a few questions?

## WHY THESE WORDS WORK

The typical hospital administrator wants maximum personal visibility within the health care industry, which he or she perceives is only possible by having complete operational control over the hospital.

In the past, the typical hospital administrator was a radiology administrator who made it to the top of the hospital by working his or her way up through the ranks. Of all the departments in the hospital, radiology was considered the best breeding ground for administrators. The radiology administrator had significant experience in managing the biggest budgets and buying the most expensive equipment. Most important, the "RA" was deeply involved in what had become one of the hospital's most vital revenue-producing services—non-invasive diagnostic imaging.

Even though he or she was "only a tech," the breakthroughs in non-invasive diagnostic imaging made the radiology administrator a relatively important person in the hospital.

The radiology administrator wasn't nearly as "important" as the radiologist, of course. But he or she was certainly more highly regarded than most other "techs" and departmental administrators.

But today, the typical hospital administrator isn't "a tech who made good."

Today's administrator is a college graduate with a degree in hospital administration. And his or her career goals are entirely different from the former type of administrator's.

Administrators used to be grateful just to be where they were. It was quite an accomplishment for someone who started off as a tech. Becoming the administrator of a hospital—even a small hospital in a small community—was a dream come true for old-style administrators.

They considered it being at the top of the pyramid. It was the culmination of a long career of working hard and paying their dues. So their goal was just to get there.

The goal of today's administrator is to get past there.

The new breed of administrator is a lot more ambitious and less loyal than the old administrators. Being the administrator of a decent-sized hospital today isn't considered the culmination of anything, much less your entire career. It's considered a dead end . . . the end of the line, vertically speaking, because you can't go any higher within the hospital. So instead of staying put and being grateful, the modern administrator thinks about moving on to a bigger playing field.

For example, the administrator of a 200-bed hospital has no higher career goals to satisfy at that institution. He or she can only advance by moving to a 500-bed hospital. And once that goal is accomplished, there's nowhere to go but out and up again. So, it's on to a 1,000-bed hospital.

They feel they must protect their careers—not the hospital—from spendthrift, self-indulgent physicians who would spend the hospital into bankruptcy if they were allowed total buying discretion.

That means administrators have to maintain control because they're convinced there are few others who can be trusted with decisions related to finances. Besides the administrators themselves, the most powerful and well-educated people in the hospital are the physicians . . . and administrators have little respect for their business judgment.

## Specific Words to Use When Selling to Hospital Administrators: Make Your Product or Service the Right Answer— No Matter What You Sell

To gain the best chance of having your product or service claims believed and accepted, position it before you begin to describe it.

### PRODUCT OR SERVICE WANT

To gain the best chance of having a hospital administrator believe and accept any product/service claim, you must carefully position your product or service before you start to describe it.

And you should position it by using words and phrases like these:

- A reasonable life cost
- Flexible
- Adaptable to all kinds of challenges
- Responsive to change

### EXAMPLE OF A PRODUCT- OR SERVICE-POSITIONING STATEMENT

- Before we discuss our [product/service], let me emphasize that it's flexible and adaptable to all kinds of challenges.

### WHY THESE WORDS WORK

As far as hospital administrators are concerned, the ideal product or service has a favorable life cost while being flexible enough so that it can adapt or be adapted to changing economic conditions.

Price as an entity unto itself is almost nonexistent for hospital administrators.

Price exists in a vacuum for them until it's translated into what's called the life cost. In other words, "How much will your product or service cost me over the course of its useful life?"

Administrators want to know exactly how big a "monthly nut" they'll have to cover if they buy your product or service, which is why many administrators demand a month-by-month pro forma projection before they make a major purchase.

They might want to know about operating costs and the impact your product or service will have on usable space, which is a major priority in today's hospitals.

They also may want to know about a number of other factors, such as service expenses, parts replacement, replenishing costs, and anything else they decide affects the life cost.

After all that, the administrator will make a judgment as to whether or not you can deliver a favorable life cost.

And what makes it favorable? That's purely a matter of the decision-maker's perceptions.

Almost every administrator you contact will have first-hand knowledge of how dramatically economic conditions can and do change . . . as they do, virtually every day.

Changes in health care are constant and sometimes dramatic. Here's a historical example: Until 1983, a hospital was reimbursed by Medicare on the basis of a percentage of the costs the hospital incurred in treating a patient. That percentage was expressed as a percentage of bed days.

So an administrator's goal was to have attending physicians order lots of expensive diagnostic tests and lots of elaborate surgeries.

In fact, the more costs the hospital incurred in relation to a patient, the more it could invoice the government, and the more profits it could make. Since the demographic pattern is for senior citizens to need hospital services in a disproportionate amount to the rest of the population, Medicare provided hospitals with a gravy train. As a result, hospitals were over-bedded and the money just kept rolling in.

That produced a financially lucrative spiral . . .

Government payments for diagnostic and surgical services contributed to big profits. The revenues were then used to buy more capital equipment, so even more of those services could be provided. And the more services you could provide, the more you could bill the government and keep the spiral going.

In addition to the Medicare bonanza, the federal government would reimburse a hospital for up to 85 percent of the purchase price and maintenance costs for capital equipment. That was done through a system of monthly invoices that were submitted by the hospital.

When reimbursing hospitals on a percentage of their bed days came to an end, so did an era in which little attention was paid to controlling costs.

If anything, the system provided huge disincentives to being cost-effective.

Cost control didn't matter because the money kept pouring in. Any sloppiness on the cost control side could be more than offset on the revenue side.

All of that changed when the federal government changed its policy from percentage-based payments to flat fees.

Instead of reimbursing a hospital a percentage of open-ended and uncontrolled costs, the government would only pay a per-patient fixed rate for each type of pathology.

For example, if a patient had a liver problem, the hospital received a flat fee that the government considered appropriate for treating a diseased liver. Of course the hospital could spend more than that, but it wouldn't get reimbursed for the difference.

So whether it makes a profit or suffers a loss depends on how well the administrator can control the hospital's costs.

How much it costs the hospital to deliver services to a patient is now just as important as how much it charges for those services.

Changes have not only taken place, but more of them are coming as the nation wrestles with the issue of health care and costs associated with it. Therefore, administrators are very conscious of cost-effectiveness in this environment.

As a result, they'll demand that your product or service be flexible enough to adapt to changing economic conditions because many administrators have learned how inflexibility can damage a promising career in hospital administration.

The good old days are over for salespeople.

At one time, all you had to do was demonstrate that your product or service would generate more revenue and you were halfway toward making a sale. But now, you have to prove a lot more.

## Specific Words to Use When Selling to Hospital Administrators: Make Your Organization the Ideal Provider

### PROVIDER WANT

To gain the best chance of having your company accepted as the ideal provider, position it before you begin to describe it.

You need to position your organization with these words:

- Marketing-oriented
- Sensitive to business requirements
- Understand what the priorities are

### EXAMPLE OF A PROVIDER-POSITIONING STATEMENT

- Allow me to tell you a few things about our marketing-oriented company. We're proud that we're sensitive to business requirements and understand what the priorities are.

### WHY THESE WORDS WORK

Every hospital administrator is vitally aware of the need for a productive DRG.

"DRG" stands for diagnosis-related group. A DRG consists of the referring physicians who—the administrator hopes—will send their patients to his hospital for tests, surgery, and other services.

To be successful—to be visible to the bigger hospitals— administrators must do a thriving business with their DRGs.

The pressure to be efficient and cost-effective has raised the importance of marketing the hospital's services.

In response to the challenge, many hospitals have formed marketing alliances. Each one agrees to specialize in a certain service within their city or region so they don't compete with each other.

By doing that, they can divide the market as partners rather than as adversaries.

You must, therefore, be perceived as having a marketing orientation. That orientation, incidentally, has nothing to do with your own marketing program. Administrators want you to be sensitive to *their* marketing priorities.

As we said before, hospital administrators believe they're virtually the only people in the hospital with a business mentality. They see themselves battling for control with self-indulgent physicians who have no true understanding of what a hospital is . . . first and foremost, it's a business.

Because they feel surrounded by a lack of financial common sense and good judgment, administrators really appreciate relationships with providers who share their view of things.

So don't make the mistake most salespeople make.

They believe the administrator is running a hospital that happens to be a business. On the contrary, administrators are running a business that happens to be a hospital.

Business priorities come first.

## Specific Words to Use When Selling to Hospital Administrators: Move Your Benefits to a Higher Level

### BENEFIT WANT

To gain the best chance of having your benefit claims believed and accepted, position them before you begin to describe them.

Describe your product or service as delivering the following benefits:

- Success on a large scale
- Significant success
- Impress the right people
- Being in the forefront with the people who matter

### EXAMPLE OF A BENEFIT-POSITIONING STATEMENT

- Our product/service offers significant success on a large scale and will impress the right people.

### WHY THESE WORDS WORK

Hospital administrators are forever seeking popularity with the referring community, the DRG. At the same time, they want to be perceived as commercially successful on a very large scale.

As we mentioned before, having appeal within the referring community is one of the most eagerly sought-after results the hospital administrator wants. Being popular with the DRG is a matter of career life or death.

If administrators had their way, they'd have professional buildings constructed right next to the hospital and filled with legions of referring physicians.

And of course, those physicians would be sending their patients to the hospital in droves.

One of the surest ways to achieve visibility and the perception of commercial success is to get splashy results on a grand scale.

In addition to the dream of the professional building next door with legions of referring physicians, is the hope of getting a large foundation grant, or a new wing on the hospital, or a profitable parking garage, or a novel way to fund the purchase of new capital equipment.

Two other indicators of success—as far as the administrator is concerned—are:

1. Fast throughput for patients who are insured by the government or HMOs. This is desirable because those patients don't represent the greatest profit opportunity. If you recall what we said before, the government has clamped down on Medicare payments by making them a flat fee. Consequently, hospital administrators would like to have those patients treated on an out-patient basis. That is, get them in and out quickly, release them early after surgery, and so on. The more bed days they occupy, the greater the chance that the hospital will lose money.

2. Heavy bedding of patients who are privately insured. Privately insured patients are a different matter. We're using the term "privately insured" to identify those patients whose insurance carriers aren't the government or HMOs, HIPCs, et al. If beds are to be occupied for a large number of patient days, administrators want them filled with patients of this type. The profit margins

are substantial and the insurance carrier doesn't have a flat rate policy.

Any one of the results we're discussing would be a boost to the administrator's career. And they're all economic in nature. Happy DRGs. Large building projects. Grants. New wings. Beds filled with the right kind of patients.

Remember, a track record that yields high visibility in the health industry begins and ends with economics. The financial pressures have reached such a critical stage in health care that no other issue takes precedence.

A hospital is successful only when it's profitable, and profitability is directly associated with the administrator . . . and no one else but the administrator.

# Specific Words to Use When Selling to Hospital Administrators: Make Your Price, Rate, or Fee a True Bargain

## PRICE, RATE, OR FEE WANT

To gain the best chance of having your price accepted, position it before you begin to quote it.

Here's how you should position your price, rate, or fee before you present it:

- Makes a high return on investment possible
- A favorable economic impact

## EXAMPLE OF A PRICE-, RATE-, OR FEE-POSITIONING STATEMENT

- Before we discuss [price/rate/fee], let me stress that it will make a high return on investment possible and will provide a favorable economic impact. I'd also like to make sure you understand everything it includes . . .

## WHY THESE WORDS WORK

As we've already discussed, the administrator is obsessed with economics because economics are directly related to personal visibility.

And a good return on investment has an obvious economic impact on the hospital.

## Specific Words to Use When Selling to Hospital Administrators: Letters and Advertising

**IN A LETTER OR E-MAIL**

Dear _____,

**Form a Special, Instant Bond:** The hospitals that run the most efficiently and effectively are the ones where the administrator is in control and stays in control. They get results that impress the people who are watching.

**Make Your Product or Service the Right Answer:** From your standpoint, therefore, no product or service serves you and the hospital better than the ones that are flexible and adaptable to all kinds of challenges.

**Make Your Organization the Ideal Provider:** And the suppliers who serve you best are marketing-oriented because they understand what your priorities are.

**Move Your Benefits to a Higher Level:** They'll help you achieve success on a large scale.

**Make Your Price a True Bargain:** And their price will make a high return on investment possible. We like to think [your product or service] and [company] can be all of that for you.

But you, of course, should be free to make that decision for yourself.

[Now, state your purpose for writing the letter, what you want the prospect to do—a call to action—communicate your normal sales message, and finish the letter.]

## IN THE FORM OF ADVERTISING COPY
### Getting Impressive Results

The hospitals that run the most efficiently and effectively are the ones where the administrator is in control and stays in control. They get results that impress the people who are watching.

From your standpoint, therefore, no product or service serves you and the hospital better than the ones that are flexible and adaptable to all kinds of challenges.

And the suppliers who serve you best are marketing-oriented because they understand what your priorities are.

They'll help you achieve success on a large scale.

And their price will make a high return on investment possible.

We like to think that [your product or service] and [company] can be all of that for you. But you, of course, should be free to make that decision for yourself.

[Communicate your normal marketing message, state what you want the prospect to do—a call to action—and finish the ad.]

**Important:** Always put these words and phrases in generic terms—as if you were describing "universal standards."

**Remember:** Their purpose is positioning. Once you communicate the Words That Sell, you can then use whatever words you normally deliver to the decision-maker about your product/service, your benefits, your company, and your price.

## Specific Words to Use When Selling to Hospital Administrators: Words That Don't Work

Avoid using these words and phrases to describe you, your company, or your product/service.

Meanwhile, use them to describe your competitors. You never have to criticize them in front of the decision-maker (which you should never, ever do in any circumstance anyway) if you know how to describe your competitors with words that don't work.

- Small
- On a small scale
- Physician-oriented
- Medicine
- A reasonable return on investment
- Work well with everyone
- Share decision-making
- Doesn't need proof
- Quiet success
- Accommodating
- Compromise
- Flexible priorities

**EXAMPLE**

- XYZ is a physician-oriented organization. They offer a reasonable return on investment, are flexible, and work well with everyone. They definitely share decision-making and can help achieve quiet success.

**WHY THESE WORDS DON'T WORK**

It's always a mistake to use negative words to describe your competitor. However, (if true) these words describe your competitor as offering the very things a hospital administrator is not looking for. Again, only use these words if they're true.

# Appendix
# 101 Universal Sales Truths

Successful selling is based on a set of sound principles, not techniques. We introduced 12 of these foundational principles in Chapter 1. It's important, however, for you to understand that there are scores of others that you need to consider as well. So here are 101 more for you to think about.*

1. Finalizing agreements and closing sales is a consequence of what has happened early in the sale rather than something the sale builds toward.
2. People buy for their own reasons, not for yours or mine.
3. Different people buy the same product or service for different reasons.
4. When a salesperson and a customer get locked into a war of wills, the salesperson always loses.
5. Buying is basically an emotional response, no matter what you're selling.
6. When people enjoy doing business with you, you're an invaluable asset.
7. If you don't close sales, you won't make a living as a salesperson.

_____

* These come from *The Universal Sales Management Truths* by Bill Brooks (Greensboro, NC: GamePlan Press, 2002).

8. Prospects must believe you before they'll buy from you! And that's a lot tougher to do than you think it is.
9. You can only convince others of what you yourself believe.
10. The more you believe in yourself, the easier it is to get others to believe what you say.
11. A strong positive self-concept is the most valuable personal attribute any salesperson can have.
12. When you believe, you can make others believe. When you don't, no one else will, either.
13. Your customer will never believe in the value of your product or service any more strongly than you do!
14. The seller determines the cost of the product or service, but only the buyer can determine its true value.
15. People pay a lot more attention to what you are than to what you say!
16. Show people what they need most in the way they want to see it, and they will move heaven and earth to get it!
17. People are always too busy to waste time doing anything they don't really want to do!
18. It is always easier to sell to a prospect's perceived need than to create need in the prospect's mind!
19. All values are equal until someone points out the difference!
20. The secret to successful selling is not in the selling at all. Instead, it is in the accurate, consistent science of prospecting.
21. The vital part of any sale is seldom the close, but what takes place before the sales interview even begins.
22. The better the job of finding qualified prospects you do, the higher your closing average will be!
23. The most productive sentence in any salesperson's vocabulary always ends with a question mark!

24. Treat prospecting as the lifeblood of your sales career—because it is.
25. You never know when your prospect's motivation to buy will suddenly and dramatically escalate.
26. The only certain way to ensure that you, your organization, or your product are thought of first is through frequent repetitious contact.
27. Constantly search for people who can give you referrals, and better yet . . . make the initial contact for you.
28. Unless you get people to lower their mental/emotional defenses and let you in, eliminate tension and establish trust, build rapport and start a successful sales dialogue, you cannot move forward to make the sale.
29. The best way to serve your own interest is to put the needs and desires of your customer first!
30. To deliver value to the prospect, you must see yourself primarily as a value resource for the prospect.
31. To be a value resource for the prospect, you must first discover what your prospect perceives as value!
32. Never interrupt a prospect. However, always be interruptible!
33. Get your whole body involved in listening and show that you are paying attention. Look the person squarely in the eye and use facial expressions and gestures to show that you hear and understand what's being said.
34. All values are considered equal in the absence of a values interpreter.
35. The fatal flaw in selling occurs when you are so focused on what you want to happen that you lose sight of what the prospect wants to happen.
36. To a prospect, any price is too high until he or she understands the value of your product or service.

37. Always tailor your presentation to the prospect's needs and wants, not to yours.
38. All sales degenerate into a struggle over price in the absence of a value interpreter!
39. Avoid making price an issue yourself.
40. A "pitch" is what is delivered from the pitcher's mound to home plate. Sales professionals don't "pitch"; they make professional sales presentations.
41. What people believe strongly enough, they act upon!
42. Never make a claim you can't back up with facts.
43. It makes little difference what you believe to be true unless you can prove it to your prospect.
44. Prospects expect salespeople to make claims for what they are selling, but they are impressed when someone else makes or endorses those claims.
45. As trust in you and confidence in the value of what you are offering rises, fear of buying disappears.
46. Always assure buyers of the wisdom of their choices.
47. Concentrate on results, not on activities.
48. True, long-lasting enthusiasm is born on the inside.
49. Enthusiasm grows when you focus on solutions and opportunities instead of problems and circumstances.
50. Most of the things that can go wrong in sales happen when a salesperson's mouth is open.
51. There are four areas where you can focus: self, company, product, or customer. If you focus on the first three, your customer is unfairly outnumbered three to one.
52. To be a top sales professional enjoying long-range success, you must be an intelligent investor of your time, talent, resources, and energies.
53. Marketing strategy is what gets you to the customer's door in the best possible light. Sales strategy is what you do when you are inside.

54. You may have to take whatever comes your way in life, but you have to go after what you want in order to be a sales winner.

55. Price alone is rarely a key factor in buying decisions. Instead, the key factor in any buying decision is the perceived value to be gained by the buyer.

56. In a crowded marketplace, all other things being equal, the one with the most information who knows how to use it wins.

57. Let your questions do the selling for you.

58. Listen people into buying instead of talking your way out of the sale.

59. Get your prospects to openly share how they feel about what they have seen and heard so you will always know where you stand.

60. Your attitude toward sales as a profession determines your selling actions.

61. When selling, connect with your own deepest values and never settle to invest a moment in anything less.

62. Salespeople who only do what they feel like doing today are bound to spend the rest of their lives unable to do what they really feel like doing.

63. Trust produces an open mind and mistrust produces a closed mind. If you gain trust, the decision-maker says, "Tell me how you can satisfy my needs" (open mind). If you achieve mistrust, the decision-maker says, "You can't satisfy my needs" (closed mind).

64. You have to address the decision-maker's emotions before you address his or her intellect. A hungry stomach cannot hear.

65. When the average decision-maker doesn't buy, he or she remembers fewer than 10 words spoken verbatim by the salesperson during the presentation.

66. The average decision-maker spends only between 9 and 20 seconds reviewing written sales materials. The average decision-maker spends only between 4 and 11 seconds reviewing a print ad.
67. The typical objection is the rational justification for an emotional decision that was made long before the objection is expressed.
68. An objection is almost always an indication that the decision-maker has a closed mind. Therefore, the objection usually has nothing to do with what caused the emotional resistance.
69. Most decision-makers are more interested in the person they're buying from than in the thing they're buying.
70. Never position yourself, your organization, or what you're selling on the basis of a feature or a benefit.
71. Successful selling amounts to making the decision-maker feel good, and being in the room when he or she does.
72. More than 80% of all salespeople talk more than is necessary to secure a sale.
73. Goals define the way you shape your own life.
74. The two main ingredients for enthusiasm are being captivated by an idea and a deep conviction that you can achieve it.
75. Compete against the achievement of your sales objectives, not against the successes of others or their expectations of you.
76. Dwell on your past sales successes. View past failures only as lessons learned and focus on the future.
77. A selling career is a continuous series of opportunities. The way we handle those opportunities is the way we handle our career.

78. Associate with positive successful people and you will be more positive and successful.
79. The secret to selling is to be in front of qualified prospects when they're ready to buy, not when you need to make a sale.
80. Take an organized approach to prospecting . . . but never at the expense of activity.
81. Never violate the formal structure of an organization . . . but master an understanding of the informal.
82. You only have a matter of seconds to establish your credibility and convince a prospect that time spent with you will be valuable.
83. Without trust you can only sell price. With trust you can sell value.
84. Focus on what the prospect is saying, not what he or she is going to say or what you're going to say.
85. When presenting price, always avoid cushioning statements like "Here we go . . . ," ""Are you ready for this?" or "Are you sitting down?"
86. Never use "set-up" statements like: "Tell me where we need to be . . . ," ""The list price is . . . ," or "I want your business so . . . . "
87. Always ensure that value exceeds price and then—and only then—present your price as related strictly to value.
88. Prospects pay attention to people they believe have something important to say to them.
89. Selling is a science that, when practiced correctly, can become an art.
90. The fear of loss is as powerful as the joy of gain.
91. The jump from character (what you are) to reputation (what people think you are) is much smaller than many salespeople would like to believe.

92. Once you discover what your prospect perceives his or her most pressing need to be, build your whole presentation around that need.

93. Value-based salespeople always concern themselves first and foremost with how the prospect perceives his or her needs.

94. Uncover your prospect's needs, as he or she perceives them, and then enable him or her to meet those needs through what you are selling.

95. Canned sales presentations are insulting to today's educated and alert consumers, many of them professional buyers.

96. Lack of qualified prospects is the greatest single cause of failure among salespeople. Prospecting is the toughest part of selling.

97. Good prospecting is a matter of developing a solid game plan that works well for you and following that game plan to the letter.

98. There is a vast difference between self-centeredness and serving your own best interest.

99. If all you want to talk about is yourself—your interests, products, features, or organization—don't be surprised if you encounter strong sales resistance from the outset.

100. What allows salespeople to be differentiated from a vending machine is that salespeople have an opportunity to meet the widely varied and specific needs of each customer they serve.

101. Listening is a skill that can be learned and can also be continuously improved, but most of us have never been trained to listen. For example, which do we do most during the day: read or listen?

# About the Authors

**Jeb Brooks** is executive vice president of The Brooks Group, an award-winning sales training firm that helps organizations improve their sales effectiveness by providing sales and sales management assessment, training, and retention services. In addition, he manages and writes for The Brooks Group's Sales Evolution Blog. Connect with him at www.LinkedIn.com/in/JebBrooks.

**William T. Brooks** (1945–2007) was the founder of The Brooks Group. An internationally recognized expert on sales and sales management, he wrote 19 books and countless articles. During his lifetime, he personally trained more than one million sales professionals in his signature IMPACT Selling System.

# The Right Phrase for
# Every Situation...Every Time

Perfect Phrases for Building Strong Teams
Perfect Phrases for Business Letters
Perfect Phrases for Business Proposals and Business Plans
Perfect Phrases for Business School Acceptance
Perfect Phrases for College Application Essays
Perfect Phrases for Cover Letters
Perfect Phrases for Customer Service
Perfect Phrases for Dealing with Difficult People
Perfect Phrases for Dealing with Difficult Situations at Work
Perfect Phrases for Documenting Employee Performance Problems
Perfect Phrases for Executive Presentations
Perfect Phrases for Landlords and Property Managers
Perfect Phrases for Law School Acceptance
Perfect Phrases for Lead Generation
Perfect Phrases for Managers and Supervisors
Perfect Phrases for Managing Your Small Business
Perfect Phrases for Medical School Acceptance
Perfect Phrases for Meetings
Perfect Phrases for Motivating and Rewarding Employees
Perfect Phrases for Negotiating Salary & Job Offers
Perfect Phrases for Perfect Hiring
Perfect Phrases for the Perfect Interview
Perfect Phrases for Performance Reviews
Perfect Phrases for Real Estate Agents & Brokers
Perfect Phrases for Resumes
Perfect Phrases for Sales and Marketing Copy
Perfect Phrases for the Sales Call
Perfect Phrases for Sales Presentations
Perfect Phrases for Setting Performance Goals
Perfect Phrases for Small Business Owners
Perfect Phrases for the TOEFL Speaking and Writing Sections
Perfect Phrases for Writing Company Announcements
Perfect Phrases for Writing Grant Proposals
Perfect Phrases in American Sign Language for Beginners
Perfect Phrases in French for Confident Travel
Perfect Phrases in German for Confident Travel
Perfect Phrases in Italian for Confident Travel
Perfect Phrases in Spanish for Confident Travel to Mexico
Perfect Phrases in Spanish for Construction
Perfect Phrases in Spanish for Gardening and Landscaping

**Visit mhprofessional.com/perfectphrases for a complete product listing.**

Learn more. Do more.